This is a very personal account of an amazing, life-changing mentor-mentee relationship of two remarkable women, written with honor and integrity. This is a story of discipleship carried out in day-to-day living, something that is rare and wonderful in today's busy world. This book tells about Sister Elvina Miller, an outstanding leader, pastor, and discipler. She touched my life as we served together in Latin America on the Alberto Mottesi Evangelistic Team. She taught, trained, empowered and launched many into more effective and purposeful lives, serving the Lord Jesus and changing their world. This writing also expresses the gratitude, appreciation, and love of one of her most outstanding disciples. It conveys a true and moving story of the passing of a bright torch of servant-leadership with a lasting legacy.

Linda Richey "Tia Linda"
Tia Linda Ministries
Santa Clarita, California

This book, like the author, is both different and unique. Woven within the fabric of these pages are truths that can change your life and set you free. It is a wonderful example of relationship; master and apprentice, mentor and student, mother and daughter. It is a modern day story of Naomi & Ruth with added detail. Pastor Nancy's honesty, transparency, truthfulness, and ability to admit and overcome her failures, have not only helped me, they have saved my life. Please read this book!

Pastor Ambrose E. Brennan III
Administrator
Oasis International Training Centre

When I look at Pastor Nancy, I see a modern-day David. She is truly a woman after God's own heart! And since I have been doing some reading about the life of David, this seems to fit, very well …

1 Samuel 16:7 NIV ***But the LORD said to Samuel, "Do not consider his appearance or his height, for I have rejected him. The LORD does not look at the things people look at. People look at the outward appearance, but the LORD looks at the heart."*** (emphasis added)

Pastor Nancy's appearance was not what attracted Bishop Miller to her … she saw beneath the exterior hippie girl and saw a heart of servitude. A heart of love and compassion. She saw something that others did not see and was willing to take the chance and invest her time and efforts into this girl from a different generation!

1 Samuel 16:15-18 NIV ***Saul's attendants said to him, "See, an evil spirit from God is tormenting you. (16) Let our lord command his servants here to search for someone who can play the harp. He will play when the evil spirit from God comes upon you, and you will feel better." (17) So Saul said to his attendants, "Find someone who plays well and bring him to me." (18) One of the servants answered, "I have seen a son of Jesse of Bethlehem who knows how to play the lyre. He is a brave man and a warrior. He speaks well and is a fine-looking man. And the LORD is with him."*** (emphasis added)

Now, I am not saying that our Bishop, my Grandma, had an evil spirit, but she did have the spirit of God in her and that spirit was pretty tough on Pastor Nancy! I know, I experienced it also, as did many of you. But through it all, Pastor Nancy (usually) kept her sweet spirit and in all things was able to see that Bishop Miller was not out to do her evil, but to get the fleshly nature out of her. And all through this, Pastor Nancy kept serving Grandma. Writing for her, cleaning for her, cooking for her, doing her laundry, etc. Whatever she could do, she would.

1 Samuel 16:21-22 NIV ***David came to Saul and entered his service. Saul liked him very much, and David became one of his armor-bearers. (22) Then Saul sent word to Jesse, saying, "Allow David to remain in my service, for I am pleased with him."***

And Grandma liked her very much and they became more than just "master and pupil", but they became friends and co-laborers. As Grandma's physical condition began to deteriorate to the point that she could not function in the same roles she once did, Pastor Nancy continued to love her and care for her like an adult child does to the parent they love. As family, we were not in a position to care for

Grandma as she needed, but Pastor Nancy never complained, never questioned, never made us feel bad about where we were or what we could or could not do. She selflessly continued to care for and protect her leader, her Bishop, her friend, her Spiritual Mother. Even to the point of neglecting her own health and well-being.

It took great patience and convincing for her to be willing to hand the care over to another, but even then she still cared and loved on Grandma. Her love for Bishop Miller was undeniable!

This book is written from that perspective. As you journey through the pages of Bishop Miller and Pastor Nancy's life together you will laugh and cry along with them, and after you are finished laughing or crying, you will pause and reflect on the lessons that have just slapped you upside the head! As you read, let the words of this book speak to your heart.

Art Speck,
Grandson of Bishop Elvina E. Miller
Senior Pastor, The Oasis of Love Church.
Huntingdon, PA
Director of the Oasis International Training Centre
Prampram, Ghana

help her

help her

MY UNUSUAL ADVENTURE AT THE SIDE OF BISHOP ELVINA E. MILLER

by Nancy A. Hudson

eGenCo

Generation Culture Transformation
Specializing in publishing for generation culture change

eGenCo
824 Tallow Hill Road
Chambersburg, PA 17202, USA
Phone: 717-461-3436
Email: info@egen.co

www.egen.co

facebook.com/egenbooks

youtube.com/egenpub

egen.co/blog

twitter.com/egen_co

instagram.com/egen.co

pinterest.com/eGenDMP

Publisher's Cataloging-in-Publication Data
Hudson, Nancy A.
Help Her. My Unusual Adventure at the Side
of Bishop Elvina E. Miller.; by Nancy A. Hudson.
Rebekah Helman, editor.
152 pages cm.
ISBN: 978-1-68019-875-1 paperback
      978-1-68019-876-8 ebook
      978-1-68019-877-5 ebook
1. Christianity. 2. Relationships. 3. Mentor.
I. Title
2017955137

Dedication

This book is humbly dedicated to two friends.
These two ladies are responsible for being "the light of Christ" and the "salt of the earth"
to me, at two extremely impressionable times in my life.

Cindy Leitzel Morlock
and
Rebecca Dixon Scott

Thank you, and thank God for you!

Bishop Elvina E. Miller, D.D.

Bishop Elvina E. Miller, D.D. was the founder and president of Deliverance Temple, Inc., which incorporates the Oasis of Love Churches and Oasis International Ministries and is based in Shippensburg. PA.

Bishop Miller and her late husband, Harrison F. Miller, were both saved in the Assembly of God Church in Hamburg, PA, where they faithfully served until they were called into full-time evangelistic ministry in the late 1940s. Bishop Miller, better known as Sister Miller in her younger years, never forgot the divine call she received shortly after her salvation. "Africa...Dark Africa...Will you go?"

While making plans to go to Africa in 1951, God intervened and the Millers found themselves pastoring a small church in Saxton, PA. That same year Sister Miller aired her first radio broadcast in the Saxton area. People who traveled from Shippensburg to Saxton to attend their meetings urged the Millers to begin services in the Shippensburg area as well. Soon it became apparent that they were to plant a church there, which they named Deliverance Temple.

The day the cornerstone was laid on the church in Shippensburg, Bishop Miller took off for her first trip to Africa, 19 years after receiving the call to the mission field. Thousands, many of whom received healing for their bodies and their souls, attended her meetings in Gold Coast (now Ghana). During this time in Africa, Sister Miller visited Prampram, a small fishing village on the coast. It was there that she was captured by Fetish priests and miraculously delivered before she was stoned. She returned to the United States in time to dedicate the Temple.

In the 1960's another field was ripening - Cuba. Sister Miller and her husband were there in the years preceding the takeover by Castro. During their time in that island country, Sister Miller preached the hope of the Gospel and warnings concerning the evils of Communism in meetings and over the airwaves that covered the entire island.

Because of what she had witnessed in Cuba, Sister Miller wanted to alert the American people and the Church to what was happening. As a result "The Voice of the Hour" radio broadcast was born and was heard on many stations in Pennsylvania and Florida.

In the early 1970's, many young people, hungry for the Word of God, found their way to Deliverance Temple. They needed instruction and guidance in the ways of the Lord, which the Millers were more than happy to provide. Unfortunately, Brother Miller passed away, leaving Sister Miller alone to train leaders to carry on the vision of reaching the lost for Jesus Christ. Still the mission field called to Bishop Miller, who traveled extensively, preaching the Gospel to thousands in many churches in Ghana, Nigeria, South Africa, Zimbabwe, Zambia, Malawi, Japan, Brazil, South America, Central America, the Caribbean islands, Puerto Rico, Canada, Italy, Greece, Hong Kong, China, The Philippines, Australia, Spain, Germany, Portugal and many other nations.

When Bishop Miller could not personally go, she was always there through the Living Word Broadcasts, which had continuously aired since the early 1980's. Thousands of letters received testify to the impact the radio broadcasts have had on lives in Africa, India, Russia, the Philippines, the United States and many other parts of the world.

During those days other churches were established, eventually named "The Oasis of Love Church". Rev. Miller received an Honorary Doctorate of Divinity in 1989 from Trinity College of Ministerial Arts in Nigeria. It was presented to her by The Rev. Macauley Nwulu, D.D., PhD. In 1999, Bishop Giacinto Beninate and a company of Elders consecrated Dr. Miller as Bishop and Overseer over the Church of the Lord Jesus Christ.

Following decades of ministry, one would think that it would be time to retire, but it was indeed time to RE-FIRE. Once again God spoke to her telling her to buy a plot of land in Prampram, the fishing village where she was captured nearly a half century ago. Thus the Oasis International Training Centre was established in Prampram, Ghana, West Africa.

Construction began in 1999; it was dedicated in 2000 and classes officially began in 2002. Since then, many students have attended the classes at the Training Centre and many have graduated. The influence of the Oasis International Training Centre is being felt in Prampram and the surrounding area as students take what they are learning to others in Ghana.

The motto of the Centre stands as: "Living to Train, Training to Live." It is a perfect description of the life-long dream and vision of the founder of The Oasis of Love Churches and Oasis International Ministries. She is one who has built, one who has sacrificed, one who has suffered, but one who has withstood it all, for the sake of the call.

After leaving Ghana for the last time at 90 years of age, in 2007, Bishop Miller returned to Shippensburg where she spent several years overseeing the churches in Pennsylvania as well as the transition of the leaders God would use to carry on her vision and His work in the Kingdom of God.

On August 2, 2016, Bishop Elvina E. Miller passed from this life, reaching her heavenly home with her Lord and Savior, Jesus Christ. There, we are sure she is dancing before the throne worshipping at His feet! Well done thou good and faithful servant, well done!

Table of Contents

Foreword

I have known Pastor Nancy Hudson for over two decades. As a present-day apostle in the Kingdom of God, I can definitely say she is peculiar. No, not strange or odd as in weird or bizarre, although for a time in her life that would have been a perfect description, but peculiar as in 1 Peter 2:9's peculiar: *a person for God's own possession*. I have observed Pastor Nancy over the many years of our joint ministries, and I can genuinely say that I have been blessed, and extremely impressed, in watching the devotion and dedication she demonstrated in serving Bishop Miller. She never sought recognition for herself and the only recompense she was interested in was the privilege of serving her oversight. And serve she did. I cannot adequately express the respect and admiration I hold toward Bishop Miller, but it is Nancy who has impressed me beyond the construction of words. I knew by the Spirit of the Lord, many years ago, that the mantle of the mentor would one day drape over the shoulders of the one called to *Help Her*. While this amazing book is first and foremost focused on the *Chronicles of Elvina*, it's also the story of a present-day Dorothy (Pastor Nancy) as she follows her yellow brick road toward her spiritual Emerald City.

I strongly recommend *Help Her* to be read by anyone who knew Bishop Miller as well as anyone who never had the privilege of witnessing that bony prophetic finger being pointed in the face of sin. Pastor Nancy's transparency allows us to see both the human and spiritual side of this great woman of God. She portrays her mentor as a one-of-a-kind servant of God who was dearly loved and respected by those who truly knew her, yet maliciously maligned by those who did not understand her God-given assignment.

Bishop Miller was appointed by God to serve as an apostle/prophet to a lost and confused generation of free-spirited beatniks and hippies. She loved the unlovely and embraced the unloved but more than that, she brought into her home and life the unlovable. There she taught them, dressed them, fed them and passionately tried to protect them from falling once again into the lifestyle that had drudged them through the murk and mire of personal and social degeneracy. She was consumed by the call to bring deliverance to the sin oppressed wherever they were on planet earth. Her disdain for spiritual pretense and her prophetic punditry were welcomed by those she ministered to, but viewed skeptically by the religious elite and cynically by the sanctified self-righteous.

I first met Sister Miller at Dr. David Minor's convention in Coudersport, PA, in 1998. As I shook the hand of this diminutive red-headed Italian preacher, I knew instantly, in my spirit, that she was an anointed prophetess of God. During the 1990 presidential campaign I invited Sister Miller to our church in Pittsburgh to join our effort in praying and working for the election of George W. Bush as President of the United States. As we sat around a luncheon table that day, and I listened to Sister Miller speak, I knew that I was in the presence of a true matriarch of present-day truth. At that moment we formed a special bond.

Bishop Miller's impact in global missions, national Christian politics and community service is still affecting the world, our nation, and local communities through the world-wide Oasis Of Love ministries and the hundreds of disciples she has personally mentored all over the world. Of all the pastoral ordinations and bishop consecratories I have been blessed to officiate, the most rewarding and fulfilling to me was the consecration of Sister Miller into the Bishopric of the Kingdom of Christ. After the ordination, I received phone calls from members of the College of Bishop's, in which I had served, and was criticized for overseeing Bishop Miller's installation because she was a woman and because of the rumors circulating about her. I challenged them to meet Bishop Miller personally and discern what spirit was in her heart. Of all the ministers whom I have been blessed to know over the more than fifty years of service in the Kingdom of God, she is one in a handful that I KNEW was a special gift that God had given to the Church for our day.

Help Her is much more than a collection of anecdotal experiences and personal musings of Pastor Nancy's forty-plus-year relationship with Bishop Miller, which in itself is a must read. It's a chronicling of a present-day Kingdom relationship in the manner of Moses and Joshua, Elijah and Elisha, Naomi and Ruth, Paul and Timothy and Jesus and John. This is the testimony of how a mighty woman of God, an authentic Biblical leader, discipled her helper so that she could become her successor. Not only will reading *Help Her* leave you feeling good, I suspect it will cause you to feel God.

Dr. George R. Beninate, Ph.D.
Bishop of Christ the King Church International
General Overseer of Abundant Life Christian Training Center, Inc.
Author of The *Jesus Strategy*, The Word of Agreement, Prophetic Worship,
Thus Saith the Lord, Age of Glory, Resurrection ~ Fact or Fiction, Showboat
Pittsburgh, PA, USA & Phnom Penh, Cambodia

Hello

Hello, friends and family! In the year 2015, I began the process of taking on this adventure. I call it an adventure because I had to sort through over 40 years of memories and try to narrow down the important from the ridiculous, the hilarious from the meaningful, and the too intimate from the "it's okay to share these facts and stories." I worked through raw emotion because during this journey, I lost my best friend, my mentor, and my pastor. I lost her first to Africa, then I lost her to old age and memory loss, and finally, the world lost her to Heaven. It has been a terror and a delight to write, and I am thrilled to complete a task she asked me to do years ago, when she was still here on earth and a vital everyday part of my life.

Bishop Elvina E. Miller was a rarity. Born in 1917, she was the daughter of immigrant Italians and was raised in a large family in Hamburg, Pennsylvania. She was a member of the Roman Catholic Church until her conversion after which she and her husband, Harrison, were sent into the ministry by her pastor. Fortunately, for those of us who are affiliated with her churches and ministry in Pennsylvania, they settled in Shippensburg, Pennsylvania and established a church. In the process, this dynamic couple led thousands to faith in Jesus Christ. That's where my generation comes in.

We were part of the "hippie harvest" during the Jesus People revival who showed up at the door of Deliverance Temple, and the door swung wide open with welcome for this motley group. Thank God!

The story you are about to read is not a biography. It is not comprehensive, nor is it chronological. It does not always list real names, and it certainly does not list every relative, friend, animal, saint, sinner, minister, missionary, or person who ever came in contact with Bishop Miller or our church. However, as closely as I can remember, and with continuous checking by those who have advised me, what you are about to read is true, I lived it… and I lived to tell it!

Because of who Bishop Miller was, what she accomplished in her life, and where she accomplished it, there is no way possible to tell her whole story. That would take a lifetime and a significant amount of money to retrace her steps around the globe. But she didn't ask me to write her whole story; rather, she asked me to write about what it was like to live with a missionary. I have written this story from my perspective as my life was intertwined with hers for a very long period of time. It was an honor and a privilege to know her, and it is an impossible task to succeed her.

Throughout this journey, you will notice a continuous change of what I choose to call her. I begin with Sister Miller. At times, I call her Bishop Elvina E. Miller, but I may also refer to her as Dr. Miller. In one chapter, she is addressed as Elvina when I refer to her relationship with a family member. These names are, however, all one and the same. The Reverend…Doctor…Bishop Elvina Elizabeth Miller. My spiritual Mom.

In my mind, there will never be another minister, lady, or person like Sister Elvina E. Miller. She was specifically chosen by God Almighty to do what she did in her lifetime, and she left this earth having completed the task at hand! Those of us who had the privilege to interact with her were better for it!

It is possible to examine with a fine-tooth comb (so the saying goes) and find fault here and there, in the way something is said, or the way it is done by *any* given individual. Those fault-finders make me smile. Take a look in the mirror, folks. When I take an honest look, I see an imperfect person, but one who is genuinely giving her best to do what God has called her to do. That being said, I loved my opportunity to live with and serve Bishop Elvina E. Miller. In her humanity, she excelled at being down-to-earth, real, and truthful—

some would say, to a fault! Through the years, she mellowed some and continued to learn, maintaining her righteous standard for God's Word and His ways, not just at the pulpit, but down where we all lived.

I hope I can do the same, that is, the mellow-and-learn part.

God asked me to "Help her." I'm still at it, Bishop Miller. I'll be doing it until I take my last breath.

Your servant,
Nancy

Acknowledgments

Many thanks are due to a multitude of people who contributed to the body of this work. First of all, thank you to Bishop Elvina E. Miller, whom I actually can't thank enough for my life. Because of her, many of the things I was destined to do, and wanted to accomplish, have come to pass. I wanted to write a cookbook, and because of her, I've written two. My goal as a child was to be a hostess. I am indeed that! In addition, Bishop Miller helped me go to etiquette school, a dream come true. I have always loved traveling, and Bishop Miller made that come to pass. She took me all over the world, sent me all over the world with others as well, paid for numerous vacations for me, and encouraged me to be a good traveller—one with patience, dignity, and manners! She taught me the Bible and spent time living it in front of me, so that I could live it in front of the next generation—a generation who doesn't need religion, but who needs the truth.

Many thanks to Bishop Miller's family. They deserve an award. Bishop Miller didn't fit the status quo of a grandmother, aunt, mom, sister—any of those titles, but she was great at wearing any and all of those hats, because she put God first and led by example. You could never deny that she truly loved you. She beamed with pride, many times from the far mission field, at every accomplishment of her kids and grandkids. Even if she couldn't be there for plays, football games, or other celebrations, she was proud of and loved each one deeply. She kept every picture you sent her and displayed them on shelves, walls, vanities, and even in her bathroom.

You, her family, are to be thanked for your love, support, prayers, and ability to be patient while she served God, many times putting her spiritual children's needs before those of her natural family. From one who benefitted from her love and mothering, THANK YOU! She saved my life! Thank you for sharing her with the world!

Thanks to everyone who supported and encouraged me as I wrote: Nancy Godfrey, Nancy and Ed Schale, Susie and Ambrose Brennan, Angelique Brown, Diane McKee, Kathy Speck, Jan Hayhurst,

Christy Schale, Lois J Schale, Art Speck, Adrienne Paey, Julianne Hayhurst, and many others. Specifically, those who listened to me read chapters and gave me feedback were so very helpful. Until I got on a roll, I kept questioning myself as to my ability to write this—especially when I was at 28,000 words and Nancy Godfrey said, "You aren't done, keep writing." Now, at over 51,000 words, she has pulled another whole book out of me! Thanks to Dex for doing one of the final edits. Thanks to Cris Miller for helping me to clarify a section.

Thank you to my family, who include some people I can't thank personally because they have gone to be with the Lord. One is my mother, Kathryn (Harpster Hudson) Breon. She was a jewel and an angel. She had zero enemies in this life. I really don't know of a sweeter person who ever lived, and she had immeasurable patience with her precocious, rebellious, stubborn daughter. She recognized my determination, and finally, she was able to find peace with the path I had followed in life. Her support meant everything to me...and I could tell her anything...and she seemed to understand. Thank you, Mom. We are...Penn State!

Thank you to my Aunt Nancy. At certain pivotal times, my precious Aunt Nancy, who has also gone to be with the Lord, was an ear to me and guided me through some rough waters while never discouraging me from my calling. During one very important turning point in my life, over lunch at the Bel-View Tavern, she, along with my mother's advice, helped me sort through some interesting decisions. I am forever grateful for her love and legacy and am honored to bear her name.

Thank you to Rick, Allison, Melanie, and Travis. I love you more than you know. Thanks for understanding me and sharing me with our congregation and for sharing me with Bishop Miller. She needed me, but I *really* needed her! I hope you enjoy this book. Rick, one time you told me, "Sometimes it's easier to write things down than say them." This is one of those times.

Thanks to our church, The Oasis of Love Church of Shippensburg. My family. Some of you have been with me for the whole trip. Some came halfway. Some detoured but got back on the road. Some are new to the journey. But whatever length of time we have known each other, I love you and appreciate your support as we travel this road together, serving our Lord Jesus Christ. This promises to be a great adventure!

Hugs and kisses!

Love,
Nancy A. Hudson

Introduction

There was a very nice crowd on hand. I was touched at how many family, friends, and those in ministry had come to support my transition into a new position of leadership. The ministry team had begun to walk down the aisle as if in a bridal procession. I likewise made my way down the aisle past friends, family, and community leaders, and into my seat. It was somewhat surreal. I am sure it is for most people who find themselves in a place that never in their craziest imagination did they think they'd be in! Back in the '70s, I would have said it was an out-of-body experience as I listened to words of encouragement, praise, blessing, and instruction spoken over me and as I became senior pastor and overseer of our fellowship of churches. Thankfully, we were way beyond the '70s!

After prayer, it was my turn to speak, and as I looked over the crowd, I thought of one person—Bishop Elvina E. Miller. As my senior pastor, Bishop, friend, and second mother for much of my life, she was the one I missed on this day. Although she was still physically with us, she was advanced in age, and having spent herself for the Gospel's sake had taken its toll on her mind and her little body. Attending this transitional service would have been impossible. Nevertheless, she was still missed.

One request she had asked me had been a simple one. As she leaned across her table one day at breakfast, I heard her say, "I had a dream about you last night." And I said, "Yes? What was it about?"

Her response didn't surprise me. "I dreamed you wrote a book about what it's like to live with a missionary. And I think you should do it."

I nodded my head in agreement, and six years later, here we are.

What is it like to live with a missionary? Or maybe I should ask, what is it like to live with a prophetess, a teacher, a lady, a woman of God, a friend, a mom, someone who was the most spiritual but truly natural, normal person I had ever known? I will attempt to share my thoughts, giving the highest regard and respect due this precious saint. At the time of this writing, Bishop Miller has just passed away at the age of 99. She'll never read this book, but in the annals of Heaven, these memories and stories are remembered, no doubt, as much for their life-changing circumstances for me as for the continual shaping of a group of believers who are having an impact for the Kingdom of God.

For me, I think it's best to begin at the beginning, and that would be the story of how we first met.

Chapter One

"GOD FIXED A FIX"—SISTER EDNA WEAVER

Lift up your eyes all around, and see: they all gather together, they come to you....
(Isaiah 60:4 NKJV)

It was the summer *after* Hurricane Agnes hit in 1972. This terrible storm had moved inland and sat right on top of central Pennsylvania for days. During the following summer in 1973, right before my second semester of my junior year of college, I was seeking employment. Jobs were terribly hard to find; our part of the state was still reeling from the effects of that previous summer's hurricane, and everyone seemed to be out of work.

I had gotten saved, become a Christian, was born-again (however you understand it), in late December of 1972, the previous winter, and returned to school after a one-semester "sabbatical." To tell the truth, I had been a drop-out. But the following spring semester was a very positive time for me as I literally saw miracles happen in my life. I had gotten born again and was allowing Jesus to begin directing my path. My life had turned around and upside down.

After my "conversion," I was still mighty "rough around the edges," but I was *trying* to change. My last hurrah that spring semester was a huge "yard sale" in front of my dorm in Salem, West Virginia (where I attended Salem College). I was attempting to sell items such as: whole subscriptions to *Mother Earth News*, rolling papers, all my "acid rock" albums, a bong, some hippie clothes, a few pipes…. (Should I go on? I didn't think so. I am sure you get the picture and realize that I was purging myself from the old.) Actually, my friend, Jane, and I needed money to go to Florida for spring break, and that was the best way I could figure out how to earn it.

Shortly after our return from a somewhat rough trip to Florida, where Jane and I didn't agree on much, I realized that if I was to stay a Christian, I'd better find some new friends. So, I slowly moved away from some of the old gang, but it wasn't easy. During the latter part of the semester, I put signs up in the elevator in our dorm that said, "I have become a Christian. I need fellowship. I live at…. Please call me at…." But they were always getting torn down. Until one day, I came home from class and found a note on my door inviting me to a fellowship meeting on campus. This opened the door for me to meet some new people, including Mrs. (Professor) Venita Zinn. If you've heard me talk about her, you'll remember she was once a child actress who appeared in the original Little Rascals movies. She was the first on a list of gifted, loving women whom God mercifully placed in my life to help guide me in my walk with God. Her home became a haven for me during an unusual and amazing time as I completed school (which is another story for another time). I say all this to lay a little ground work for my meeting with Bishop Miller and how it came to be.

That summer (again, it was 1973), I "rolled into Dodge" (my hometown of Lewistown, Pennsylvania), ready to rumble and did nothing but run to church meetings for the first few weeks at home. Finally, my wise mother, Kathryn Hudson, asked me what I was planning to do all summer. I knew that meant I had better find a job, and I also knew they were hard to find. So on the advice of my peers, I took a job at the local kosher chicken plant where many of my friends who had gotten saved were also working. The ultimate goal was to get all the rabbis to convert! That sounded good to me, and since a friend of mine told me to take the job, I did. After all, she had just prayed for her broken-down car to start, and it had started! I knew it had to be God listening to her! It just so happened that taking the job would be His perfect direction.

I hate to take much of your time telling you this piece of my history, but without it, I don't know if you can get the picture of how miraculously God led me to Elvina E. Miller and Deliverance Temple. So here goes.

My first day at the kosher chicken plant was also my last. I had never touched a dead chicken in my life, nor did I plan to. I am not sure how I thought I would survive in a warehouse that had nothing but *thousands* of dead chickens flying all around, attached to conveyor belts, where at various "stations" people would "do things" to them.

That day I made my rounds at various jobs. I think the supervisors were trying to figure out what this "spoiled little brat" could or would actually do! I burned pin feathers off of the chickens. I plucked pin feathers. I threw chickens into a moving bin. I bagged chickens. And hours later, although I wore the assigned goggles and a special jacket, I had chicken juice all over me! Did I mention that the pungent, horrendous smell of that chicken juice was *everywhere,* and you could not escape it no matter what you did?

I made it until the second break during the afternoon at which time I went into my boss's office and frankly told him something he already knew—this job was not my cup of chicken soup! He told me I could keep the two jackets they had given me as well as the goggles, and I headed out to wait for my friends in their van until the end of the work day. Somehow, I knew my mother would kill me when she found out I had quit, but God knew just what "fix" to fix me with, to get me to where I needed to be. Thankfully, that "fix" had nothing to do with kosher chickens!

That van became a holy place that day. I sought God's face the way that only a new Christian could, with no religious ceremony, but just the simple truth. "Lord Jesus, *help*! I *cannot* work here. You know it, Lord. *Please* find me another job." I prayed it over and over again, tears mixed with chicken juice sweeping down my cheeks. Soon my friends arrived, and we journeyed home.

The next day I was talking with another dear, godly woman, whom God had placed in my life—Grace Libby (now McKee). Her husband just happened to be in charge of the local Pennsylvania state employment agency in our town. She said, "Call Jack Libby. He'll help you find a job." I did, and sure enough, he did.

It wasn't long until I was packing my bags to begin a new job as a lifeguard/canteen operator at a local Lion's Club sponsored camp—Beacon Lodge Camp for the Blind. At the camp, I had off one day a week but lived full-time on the grounds because I was also in charge of a whole group of campers. The day after I was hired, one of my dearest friends, Becky, also was hired to do the same job, and we worked the whole summer together. Becky and I also went to college together, and she was the one who had led me to the Lord at Mom Gerhart's Pizza Shop one winter night in late 1972.

That summer of 1973 we met a lot of characters—nuns, priests, hippies (I tried to stay away from them), volunteers, college and high school students—all of whom had also been hired to be counselors or workers at the camp. It was a *great* summer. There was an adult camp and a children's camp, and one of the young people, a counselor, whom I met that summer, became my natural link to meeting Bishop Elvina Miller. He was a nice-looking local guy, a Christian, who played guitar. We got "bit by the romance bug," and before long, we were spending our days off together, as much as we could. We would visit his family, my family, and at some time right before the summer ended, we took a fateful trip.

He had often talked about the church he attended in Shippensburg (where he was a college student) and its loyal and dynamic pastors, Brother and Sister Miller. I listened as he talked, but not with any real interest. Now, don't get me wrong—I wanted to meet them; but at that point in life, I was envisioning marriage, 12 kids, and living happily ever after. You know—pregnant and barefoot stuff. Eventually, we planned a trip to Gettysburg and Shippensburg, of which I had no real excitement; I just wanted to be with Jim. But did that ever change in a hurry!

After a short tour and lunch in Gettysburg, we arrived in Shippensburg and drove down Washington Street, to a dead end and to this huge building. I also noticed two huge fields of weeds and another two buildings, built in a similar fashion, parallel to each other. Actually, I had never seen a church like this before. It looked like a bowling alley, with a flat top. The building did have one thing I loved—the color red—*red* doors, *red* pillars, and a *red* banister that led to a basement with *red* geraniums planted all around the basement entrance. We rang the doorbell, and this adorable lady answered. She was adorned with a pink and white dress and John Lennon glasses. She looked to be about 4 foot, 11 inches tall, but maybe that was because her hair was styled in this amazing black beehive, bigger and fancier than I had ever seen on anyone. Jim introduced me. *This* was Sister Miller.

She welcomed us in and embraced us, offering us something to drink. She was very open and hospitable. I was overwhelmed, yet not threatened by her joyous excitement and honest love for Jesus Christ. She never batted an eye when she saw me, but later in years, she shared her true feelings with me. God bless her for not running the other direction!

I had "dressed up" for the day; after all, it was a date. I wore my hair up in a very scraggly bun. In those days, it was cool to have strands of hair falling out of the bun everywhere, almost like you had slept on it for a week. I wore hip-hugger jeans with my belly button showing, and I was also "decked out" with a see-through, pink crocheted tank top, and no bra. Did I mention my black fingernails were about two inches long, and I also wore purple-shaded glasses with rhinestones around the frames, which looked like I had chased Elton John down and stolen them from him? Still, Sister Miller never flinched. Like I said, God bless her!

Sister Miller flitted around the basement of the church, giving me a quickie tour, and then she took us into a bedroom (in a church?) where she set up a film strip projector to show us her pictures from "Jesus '73," one of the first Jesus Festivals in Morgantown, Pennsylvania. She was all excited! I had heard of it, but didn't know anyone who actually had gone to it. I assumed that type of event was just for converted hippies, not someone who looked like her. I was a little puzzled that she had been there. She oohed and aahed over all the Bible teachers who had attended the festival and how exciting it was to see so many young people hungry for the Lord. After listening to her, I was seriously beginning to doubt my own salvation. Whatever she had, I wanted it! But we had to be on our way, and soon, it was time to say goodbye. But when we did, something extraordinary happened to me, something I will never forget.

Sister Miller hugged me goodbye, and when she did, she prayed a simple prayer for me while gently rubbing my back. Then she let go of the embrace. Next, she held both of my arms and looked me square in the eyes as she said these words: "Don't worry. Things aren't going to turn out the way you think they are. God has something very special in store for you. You just wait and see." Her eyes glimmered, and she hugged me again. I felt like I had been translated to Heaven! I was engulfed with God's holy presence, and I floated out the door. It was amazing!

As soon as I got into the car, I began to give Jim a piece of my mind! Why had he waited all summer to introduce me to this amazing woman of God? I can only imagine, he may have been afraid of what *she* thought of me, which could have been the reason for his hesitation. Nevertheless, I had met her, and my life would never be the same!

That was my first encounter with Sister Miller. Yep, I wanted what she had, but I wondered if I would have the stuff it took to get it. What made this lady tick? What would it be like to live, day in and day out, with this little powerhouse for God called "Sister Miller"? Time would tell, and I was about to find out!

Me - Junior Year of College

I may have touched that chicken!

This is it folks, the Kosher Chicken Plant

Beacon Lodge

The Main Building at Beacon Lodge

Sister Miller at the Kitchen Entrance

Chapter Two

HELP HER

…Your sons shall come from afar, and your daughters shall be nursed at your side.
(Isaiah 60:4 NKJV)

After that God-moment at my first meeting with Sister Miller in the summer of 1973, and because of my continued relationship with Jim, I soon had other opportunities to be around her. I remember some of my affection for her was short-lived, because my very "dominant" human nature was all too soon confronted with the God-nature alive in Bishop Miller. In other words, we clashed, because I often wanted my way, as opposed to her godly authority, something I had rarely encountered.

I'll try to describe what was going on inside of me. Have you ever met someone who continuously was fired from jobs, and according to that individual, it was *never* their fault? Rather, the problem was with the boss, or this person was misunderstood. It was always something or someone else; but this particular person was *never* at fault. That was me. Not the "getting fired" part, but I did have the mind-set that I was always right and everyone else was wrong. Now, I had met my match! She was just what I needed; I just didn't know I needed her…*yet*!

But no worries, when I visited the Temple, as it was called then, she was not always around. For that I was thankful! One early memory that stands out involves a weekend meeting. Brother Miller was conducting the worship service when he announced that he had received a tape from Sister Miller. Jim had told me she was in Africa, and to be honest, it sounded to me like she was away a lot. Of course, I had never heard of pastors taking off and going to Africa. The only time our pastor at home took off was for a month in the summer, and his family always went "down the shore." But to *Africa*…?

So, Brother Miller, with Jim's help, got the tape ready to play. And when they flipped on the switch, I certainly was not prepared for what I was about to hear. To me, it sounded like *wild* and *crazy* loud music, wilder than any Black Sabbath or Rolling Stone music I had *ever* heard! And there, *screaming* over the music was whom I assumed to be Sister Miller trying to explain what all was happening in that meeting in Africa. The sounds that came out of that recording were actually the joyous sounds of the beautiful African people, tens of thousands strong, singing blissfully in their native tongue, rejoicing in Jesus, their Savior. Also along with the singing was the majestic beating of drums. I would eventually discover there was nothing to be afraid of. It was a spectacular event!

But in that moment, while everyone in the service was thrilled with what they were hearing, I was completely horrified and scared to *death*! It was just too much for a small-town, uncultured girl! Just the thought of Africa made this ignorant soul shudder! I had never heard music like this...ever, and unfortunately got the wrong impression of my first African experience.

After that, and because of other encounters where my human nature was tested beyond what I had ever experienced from authority figures such as parents, teachers, and bosses, I informed Jim that I would never be back again to *that* church. I was scared spit-less at the power that I heard on that tape, in the form of Sister Miller, and my flesh (human nature) wanted no part of it. Sister Miller never said or did anything back then to make me feel afraid or threatened, but I suppose because I always wanted things "my way," I was threatened by her. I guess, secretly, I hoped that Jim would be whisked away by his love for me, and we could gravitate elsewhere to continue our relationship and serve God at a church that was far less "demanding." But that didn't happen.

Let me explain further. Everything was all about me. I wanted time with Jim, and time to do my thing. I didn't want to spend my spare time in prayer meetings, at the church, and other religious activities. I wanted to run around, go to lunch, go shopping, hiking, make quilts, attend sporting events, watch TV, and so on. I did love Jesus and loved what He was doing in my life, but if plans changed and I didn't get my way, I had an attitude. When enough of those attitudes built up, I would have an explosion, which usually resulted in lots of tears and pouting. I was trying to get attention, I guess. At the same time, I was always careful not to have any meltdowns around Sister Miller, but when that stuff is in you, you will slip up from time to time. Thankfully, Jim stood his ground, and within days, I would recant and be back making occasional visits to Shippensburg, whenever I could while I was attending college. I guess in some ways, I was a volcano on the verge of eruption, and it would continue to happen in times to come.

I believe Bishop Miller knew I was a tender plant. Although she spoke the truth as she guided me, she also used a certain patience that allowed me some grace while I continued to be molded and shaped into what God eventually was calling me to do. It's hard for me to remember the details during this time; but I do recall that as unlearned as I was in the things pertaining to serving God, I knew I needed to be re-baptized. I had been baptized as a baby, and baptized again in the Burnham Church of the Brethren after I received Jesus as my Lord; but after hearing Brother and Sister Miller's teaching on baptism, I was fully convinced my original baptism needed to be reinforced.

"According to your faith, so be it." (See Matthew 9:29) So, Sister Miller and Brother Miller agreed to re-baptize me for the circumcision of the heart!

> *In Him you were also circumcised with a circumcision not performed by human hands. Your whole self ruled by the flesh was put off when you were circumcised by Christ, having been buried with Him in baptism, in which you were also raised with Him through your faith in the working of God, who raised Him from the dead. When you were dead in your sins and in the uncircumcision of your flesh, God made you alive with Christ. He forgave us all our sins, having canceled the charge of our legal indebtedness, which stood against us and condemned us; He has taken it away, nailing it to the cross. And having disarmed the powers and authorities, He made a public spectacle of them, triumphing over them by the cross* (Colossians 2:11-15 NIV).

Several other people also needed to be baptized; but the only place we could go was Big Pond, and it was early April and *cold* outside! I am not sure why, but they saved me for last. When it was my turn, Brother Miller lovingly lowered me into those freezing cold waters, and when I came out, I came out the "Acts way"—speaking in tongues and prophesying!

Paul said, "John's baptism was a baptism of repentance. He told the people to believe in the One coming after him, that is, in Jesus." On hearing this, they were baptized in the name of the Lord Jesus. When Paul placed his hands on them, the Holy Spirit came on them, and they spoke in tongues and prophesied. There were about twelve men in all (Acts 19:4-7 NIV). After that, Sister Miller spoke a directional, anointed word over me, and it would stay with me my whole life. She imparted "her mantle" (that was the phrase she used) to me, and everyone who was there that day knew we all had witnessed something sovereign, something we all would talk about again and again. God had bonded me with this gracious saint, and some of what she had was given to me at that time.

Soon, it would be summer, and I had a choice to make that involved my education. When I had dropped out of school for a semester in 1972, I had missed some classes that I was required to take before student teaching. One was a human development class, and I needed to complete it by September. I was in a pickle. I did not want to be at home in Mifflin County, yet I did. I wasn't actually sure I could handle the temptation of being there around all the "old gang," yet there was a part of me that was being pulled in that direction. Penn State was offering the class, State College was close to home, and I was already registered.

Meanwhile, during those days, Sister Miller would sit on an old metal porch glider (that we still have!) in the furnace room in the basement of the church, pretty much year round, and study. So I approached her there and explained my dilemma. I guess I expected her to just tell me to "do what I had to do," but instead, she looked up from her study and said, "Did you see if Shippensburg offers the class?" Well, I had never thought of that, and to my surprise, I discovered it was offered. I was admitted, and on top of that, I found a job on campus in the printing department.

Now, because I was headed to Shippensburg for the summer to live at "Shiloh" (the name we "lovingly" called our apartment on North Washington Street) with several other girls from the church, I asked if anyone could travel to Salem, West Virginia, to help me drag all my stuff to Shippensburg for the summer. What a blessing when I found out Brother and Sister Miller would drive to Salem, help me load up my things, and follow me to Shippensburg! They arrived on a Friday night in West Virginia, stayed in a hotel, then came to see me on Saturday. We had lunch, and I gave them a tour around campus. Then they met some of my friends before we packed up my huge pile of belongings and my pet chinchilla, Eleanor (who was named after Eleanor Roosevelt), and we headed up the road to Pennsylvania. There I would begin quite an adventurous season, one that set the tone for my life.

That summer, I rode my bike to school every day at Shippensburg State College, attended my class, worked as little as possible, and then ran back to the church as soon as I could, so I could do whatever. One day, while riding my bike back from the campus, I had an experience sort of like Paul being knocked off his horse! It was a divine visitation, and I *know* it was an impression from God. I heard two words: *"Help her."* And I almost fell off my bicycle.

I was already planning on helping Sister Miller that day, but this *"Help her"* was different, like "This is your calling—*Help her*—this is what you are going to do in life—*Help her*." I was shaking and very emotional, and I went right to the church and got busy. I'm still doing that one simple chore today. First Kings 19:12 says that God wasn't in the big stuff, but He was in the still, small voice. And that was exactly what I heard—two words that set the course for my life. *"Help her."*

> *Then He said, "Go out, and stand on the mountain before the Lord." And behold, the Lord passed by, and a great and strong wind tore into the mountains and broke the rocks in pieces before the Lord, but the Lord was not in the wind; and after the wind an earthquake, but the Lord was not in the earthquake; and after the earthquake a fire, but the Lord was not in the fire; and after the fire a still small voice* (1 Kings 19:11-12 NKJV).

I hope I never forget the importance of that one simple direction from God.

Back in those days, those two words, "Help her" were fun words! "Help her" meant: painting, assisting with the cooking, walking the dog, and sewing. It meant serving Brother Miller breakfast and lunch. Because Bishop Miller often had things to attend to and had to slip out of the building for a moment, and because Brother Miller was on an odd work schedule, she would ask me at times to take care of him. Of course, since I didn't know how to do anything, poor Sister Miller had to start from scratch. She showed me how to scramble eggs, make his toast and butter it, and how he drank his coffee. Then she even showed me how to make a proper sandwich for him and what to serve with it. It seemed like they ate a lot of eggs! Little did "ignorant me" know, that eggs were what they had, so that was what they ate. Never in a million years did I ever get the impression that they had very little money, but I eventually found out that was the case.

I remember being so nervous serving Brother Miller. I'm not sure why, but I knew Sister Miller was *very* particular, and I did not want to make a mistake! Another thing I learned—we were *always* to use a cloth napkin!

I guess I should admit that that phrase "Help her" was almost a joke at times. When I honestly look back to determine how much help I was to her, things are actually the other way around! She was helping *me*. For most of the things that she wanted me to do that summer, she had to spend hours teaching me how to do.

I fondly remember the day she asked me to paint picnic tables. She gave me the paint, the brush, and a cloth to collect any drippings, and showed me where to paint. To me, this was a no-brainer, and I could handle it. So I began to paint. I figured I would start at the bottom and sat down Indian style and went to town! I painted away, and after about an hour had gone by, Sister Miller came out to check on me. There I was, painting *underneath* the table, with paint dripping all over me. *What a mess!* (to quote Tommy Lee Jones and a favorite line from the movie "The Fugitive"). Needless to say, we had a teaching moment!

Another one of my more memorable moments involves an episode as I was gardening. I had been saved for about "an hour" by then, and particularly that summer, we gardened. And it was hot! *Didn't these people believe in swimming pools, sunbathing, drive-in movies, riding in a convertible, throwing down a cold one to cool off?* I thought. Obviously not, because no one ever mentioned it. Instead, we worked in the garden during the summertime, and it was blasting hot!

Don't forget, all these chores were done with the joyful enthusiasm of new believers. We all wanted something to put our hands to that would contribute to our church and helping someone, especially our pastors at that point in time.

However, in my mind, the only thing good about gardening was that *Mother Earth News* always had great articles about farming and living off the land, and I was hoping to be able to do that someday. (*Right!*) There just had to be an easier way than weeding under the deathly hot sun! So, one particular day, I decided to do it *my* way. I came fully ready to dive into the work, Nancy-style, fully lathered with suntan oil, dressed in a halter top tied around my back and neck, short-shorts, and flip flops. I was weeding away, when I think I had either an epiphany or a true religious experience. All of a sudden, I felt naked! I felt like Adam and Eve—I was embarrassed. I was horrified and knew that I immediately had to go put on some clothes...*now*!

I jumped up, didn't say a word, and soon returned fully clothed and in my right mind. Wow, that was sovereign! No one told me to change. No one said anything. It was a God-moment. As I worked at my weeding that day, I did so, not knowing what had happened to me, but with tears rolling down my face with thanksgiving. There was something indecent or irreverent or unholy about my attitude, which was reflected in the way I was dressed. And I felt it, I knew it. Actually, in that moment, I experienced an inward change!

"Help her" also meant driving Sister Miller to various places, or accepting driving assignments on her behalf—and that's where I learned some of my greatest lessons. That summer, we had changed dates for our Conference to the July 4th weekend in order to accommodate the campus Christian fellowship group. Ed Schale was one of the many students who was here for the summer, and who ultimately, while not

from this area, ended up settling here and became part of our church, called at that time, Deliverance Temple.

I have to share at least one story about Pastor Ed, as he is now called. I remember that one of the Conference meetings was held in the basement of the church. It was an afternoon teaching session. One of my driving assignments was to drive with another student to Hamburg, Pennsylvania, to pick up Sister Miller's sister, Sundena, so she could also attend the Conference for two days. Because of that trip, we were a little late for the afternoon session and had to sit near the door. I remember during the session, Ed and another student named "David" came through the door, moved through the crowd while the speaker was speaking, summoned another young student, and they all left. (In my mind, "Elvis has left the building!")

About an hour and a half later, the meeting adjourned, and we all were fellowshipping and having some refreshments when in came Ed, "David," and "Jack" (the other student). Each of them had a soaking wet head. Ed and "David," as "campus elders," had taken "Jack" out to Big Pond right in the middle of the Conference and baptized him. With elders, prophets, and pastors everywhere, God had chosen them (tongue in cheek), in their minds, to interrupt the whole convention and perform a baptism.

What a riot! Do you understand what Bishop Miller had to work with? We had no clue that God had an order of authority. We were probably the *last* ones who should have been baptizing anyone! It was kind of like the blind leading the blind! Or perhaps it was like having a four-year-old perform open-heart surgery! Just because we had become Christians and 20 people were "following us" in a campus fellowship did not give us the authority or wisdom to baptize someone, especially while there was appointed, anointed, and ordained leadership all over the place. Sister Miller had her hands full attempting to train us in the ways of the Lord. God help her!

That was the last Conference held in which Brother Harrison F. Miller was in attendance. Although it was not known at the time, he had only a few months to live. My time with and exposure to Brother Miller's ministry and personality were limited, but I was thankful that I had been given a small slot of time to get to know him. I likewise know that he was the consummate support to Bishop Miller's somewhat over-shadowing and dominant anointing in the ministry. It was obvious that they were very much in love, and it was also obvious that he was the supporting cast member and was happy to be that person. The truth is, Brother Miller was "the brains behind the brawn," if that makes any sense. He was a fabulous organizer, a great businessman, who exhibited a gentle teaching spirit and a wonderful laugh that endeared you to his gentle ways. He loved seeing all the young people stream into the church and would do whatever it took to facilitate the move of God that was in full swing!

Two experiences totally stand out to me about Brother Miller. One time on my way back from my hometown to West Virginia where I was attending school at that time, I stopped by the Temple in Shippensburg, in the middle of the week, to say hi and to stay overnight before traveling on. I had been recently admitted to the hospital in my hometown, due to a serious asthma attack, and was still recovering. Brother Miller gently suggested that I should stay for a Bible study where he would be teaching on divine health and healing. I stayed and was fascinated by his simple demeanor and kind teaching style. He broke open God's Word, reassuring us that according to the Scriptures, healing is a provision from God.

> *Bless the Lord, O my soul; and all that is within me, bless His holy name!*
> *Bless the Lord, O my soul, and forget not all His benefits: who forgives all your iniquities, who heals all your diseases* (Psalm 103:1-3 NKJV).

> *And He entered the synagogue again, and a man was there who had a withered hand. So they watched Him closely, whether He would heal him on the Sabbath, so that they might accuse Him. And He said to the man who had the withered hand, "Step forward." Then He said to them, "Is it lawful on the Sabbath to do good or to do evil, to save life or to kill?" But they kept silent. And when He had looked around at them with anger, being grieved by the hardness of their hearts, He said to the man, "Stretch out your hand. And he stretched it out, and his hand was restored as whole as the other"* (Mark 3:1-5 NKJV).

> *He sent His word and healed them, and delivered them from their destructions* (Psalm 107:20 NKJV).

Many other Scriptures confirm that Jesus' Word heals. I asked for prayer for the troubling asthma and allergies, and that asthma attack was my last. I still struggle with some seasonal allergies and a severe cat allergy, which causes me to remember the miracle God did for me. But it also assures me that cats must have come from the curse in Genesis (sorry to all you cat lovers)!

Another trait that I remember about Brother Miller was that he was a visionary. That same particular summer, our church had been invited by the owner of a local radio station to participate in the Shippensburg Fair. Brother Miller and Ward Wiser pulled together their money and purchased a pair of speakers and a small amplifier so that we could sing and be heard as we preached the Gospel at the Fair. It truly showed his heart of outreach, his position as a pillar, and his delight at seeing this evangelistic outreach come to pass as well as succeed.

While we are on the subject, let's talk about our Fair experience that blessed summer!

After we received an invitation to be part of the Fair and noticed Bishop Miller's excitement to do it, there was no turning back! It was an opportunity to "get out there" in our local community and do what all Christians are called to do—preach the Good News! I can tell you from my perspective, I would have rather been stricken with the bubonic plague than stand in front of the whole town and sing and give my testimony! But seemingly, there was no way out of it.

Soon, we set up a small camping tent for supplies, sat on blankets in front of the tent, like we were at Woodstock, and sang. Thinking back, it must have looked ridiculous! Sister Miller left us alone for a while, then she *made* us stand up and use two microphones, those *huge* ones that were used on the radio "back in the day." I would have never defied her, but I seriously *hated* every second of those first few days. By day four, I was still hoping I would come down with something that would get me out of this perfect humiliation, but it didn't happen. I guess there may have been about 15 to 20 of us at the time, and we sang each night from four to five hours straight. On occasion, someone would share a testimony.

Knowing that to "save face" I had to show up for this "Fair" thing, I did; and during the final three days, it really wasn't that bad. I sang a few solos, and I was starting to envision myself as some type of successful "Christian" Joni Mitchell, and that actually kind of appealed to me. Plus, I have to admit that there was a growing excitement at knowing what we were doing. Out of a town of more than 35 churches, we were the only church that was on the grounds of the Fair, sharing the Gospel of Jesus Christ, and not hosting a food booth! I realize now that without the input and sacrifice of Brother Miller and Ward Wiser, our Fair ministry would have never gotten "off the ground," so to speak. I think each of those early pioneers from our church were so excited to have new blood, that they would have done anything to enable us to do what God had called us to do. And we still are doing it—more than 40 years later.

I finished my class that summer at Shippensburg State College, and before I headed back south to school in West Virginia, Sister Miller invited me for dinner and said she was making spaghetti. I was all about that, so I showed up, car packed and ready to hit the trail. When I walked in the door, I noticed that in her typically thoughtful Sister Miller way, she had organized the dinner as a send-off, thank-you, we-love-you dinner, just for me. The other guests had signed a white paper tablecloth, and I was overwhelmed and overjoyed at her continued unique and thoughtfully hospitable way.

What a way to head back for my last and most trying semester *ever* of college! During that time, I was also employed as a resident assistant (RA) and was responsible for desk duties twice a month, which put a serious crimp in my travel plans back and forth to Shippensburg. I was also student teaching in addition to taking almost a full load of classes so that I could graduate early. This meant attending Sculpture, Advanced Painting, Directing (to complete my double major) classes, and taking a class by exam…plus directing the high school play!

As a reminder to those reading this account, when I got saved, my life did a total 180! My grades went from pathetic to Dean's List, and my reputation on campus must have scared people. I am positive they did not know what to do with me, as evidenced by some of the things that went down. Some thought I was a "narc" (an undercover drug police person). Others thought I was a saint. I was actually somewhere in between!

Previously, during the semester after I received Jesus as Lord, I had been called into the Dean of Students office. At the time, I thought I was in trouble; I was so used to being paranoid from sneaking around in the drug culture. Remember, I had just met the Lord Jesus and Sister Miller—everything seemed to be changing in my life everywhere. During this meeting with Dean Davis, I was offered the RA position on the sixth floor. My dorm Super and the Dean looked me square in the eyes and said, "Nancy, you are not in trouble. [Whew!] We've seen what has happened in your life. We think you are the only one that can do that job—it's a rough floor." I called my mom to get her advice, but it was really a no-brainer. It was free room and board! But again…talk about a major disruption to my trips to Shippensburg.

Nevertheless, every weekend during which I had two spare days, I was in my VW bug and on my way to Shippensburg—six hours one way. To be honest with you, by that time, I was close to being engaged to Jim, but he was no longer the main attraction. I loved being at our church. I loved the way it was set up—so "unreligious," and there were a lot of kids my age—only a few hippie types, but that was okay. I had enough people to identify with!

I would arrive at Shippensburg on Friday nights and attend a Bible study or prayer meeting, if I got there in time. Then I would stay with one of the girls somewhere or stay in the church. On Saturdays, Sister Miller and Brother Miller would spend the day together away from the church, go for supplies, or have dinner somewhere (to get away from us). Then, Saturday nights, we would gather together, pray, read, and sing. It was kind of like communal living, but we weren't "living" together. Perhaps it was more like a Christian kibbutz. We all contributed to pay for food, which only made sense—we were eating it. Then on Sundays, we attended three services—one in the morning, one in the afternoon, one at night. Sister Miller would beg me to leave in the afternoon, but I didn't want to miss anything. So, usually around 9:00 or 9:30 p.m., I would pack my car and head down the road to Salem, West Virginia, where I would arrive in time to get ready for my student-teaching classes, take a shower, go to breakfast at 7 a.m., and then head to the school where I was student teaching. Then I would return from classes to the dorm and sleep!

Many times during my trip, while driving the mountainous roads to Morgantown, West Virginia, in my mind's eye I would see a deer. For some reason, that "vision" would alert me to pay attention and slow down. Sure enough, minutes later, there would be a deer, or two, three, or four standing along that road, ready to leap into my path. I believe God, again, sovereignly protected me, causing me to be on high alert! Another time (and this will seem hard to believe), during the gas rationing days of the 1970s, I was headed to Shippensburg on one-fourth of a tank of gas. It was not my usual day to get gas, and I actually left West Virginia unaware that my tank was so low. Sometime as I was driving, however, I noticed how low it was. For some reason (*God*), I did not panic, but continued to drive. My gas indicator never went down the whole trip—I know it was a miracle. Believe it or not, it happened. I will never forget it, and I can still remember the tears streaming down my face as I drove.

During that semester, I would get so homesick for Shippensburg, and Sister Miller's loving acts didn't make it any easier. When I couldn't be there for the weekend, the kids at the church would make cassette tapes for me. I loved when I would get them, with Sister Miller encouraging me in my faith and everyone singing songs and telling me they missed me. Many times, Shippensburg would seem like a million miles away, and I would listen to the tapes and sit and cry. One time, I got so emotional, I called off work the whole weekend, packed my bag, and headed there. I'm not sure if I mentioned this already, but it was a tough row to hoe in college after I got saved; and the encouragement, fellowship, and friendship I received from the church in Shippensburg literally got me through that very crazy year of college. During that time, I slowly separated myself from all the entanglements of my past college life, and these new acquaintances really added "muscle" to my faith, making it easier to stand for what I believed. That was an unforgettable semester.

At the same time, early during that school year, Brother Miller began really failing, yet we didn't know what was wrong with him. But although he was not well, he again encouraged Sister Miller to take a trip she had been planning to Brazil and the Dominican Republic. Subsequently, during the middle of the trip when Brother Miller became very ill, we tried to contact her in several locations, – even sending a telegram, but to no avail. Finally, God had His way and miraculously told Sister Miller to close the meeting in the Dominican Republic and come home. She obeyed and God spoke to her on the plane, revealing that Brother Miller had cancer of the bone, and He was going to take him home to Heaven.

When Sister Miller arrived home, of course, she prayed for her husband, and she immediately sought medical help. Previously, he had seen a doctor who had diagnosed his pain as a back injury. Brother Miller assumed the diagnosis was correct, for he had experienced that same pain before. When Sister Miller finally arrived home, he was almost bedfast, and the doctor admitted him to the hospital where tests confirmed the diagnosis that God spoke to Sister Miller on the plane. He had cancer of the bone, and God would be taking him home to Heaven.

Again, I travelled north to be with everyone while Sister Miller sat at Brother Miller's side. One by one, he requested to speak to each of us. I remember staying with him one night while Sister Miller took a break. He was in severe pain but had the fortitude to encourage me and tell me to serve the Lord. "Nancy," he said, "there is nothing better."

On October 12, 1974, Brother Miller went home to be with Jesus, and Sister Miller was left alone with a church full of kids. When she asked God for help in the ministry, I am sure this is not what she bargained for. Even so, out of that group would come forth the nucleus of people who are the pillars of our church today. Nothing is too difficult for God!

Sister Miller preaching to thousands in Ghana - early 1950's

Part of the crowd in Ghana

18

Brother and Sister Miller

Part of the infamous garden

Another shot of the other half of the garden

Early days of the Shippensburg Fair

Very early Fair picture

Brother and Sister Miller early 70's

Chapter Three

THINGS AREN'T GOING TO TURN OUT THE WAY YOU THINK THEY ARE

The sons of foreigners shall build up your walls, and their kings shall minister to you; for in
My wrath I struck you, but in My favor I have had mercy on you.
(Isaiah 60:10 NKJV)

It was the beginning of the winter of 1974. Finally, I would graduate from college, and I knew where I wanted to move. But I had to have a job. One thing I did have was faith and friends in the right places. At that time, Nancy (Gerfen) Godfrey worked at the local newspaper, *News-Chronicle,* and one of her "beats" was to report on the school board meetings. On one of my many trips back to Shippensburg, Nancy was thrilled to tell me the news that a position had opened up for an art teacher at the Shippensburg Junior High School. It was a six-month sabbatical position, filling in for a teacher who was close to retiring. Immediately, I gathered my "unfinished" resumé along with a completed application, and submitted the material before the open position hit the papers.

One week later, I had an interview, and on the day that I completed college, I ran to the campus post office one last time. There was my job offer from Shippensburg School District. I was already packed to move, and now I had my "reason" to move! With no time to call anyone and no cell phones in those days, I was getting out-a-there, and never looked back. That life was over, and I knew it. I wasn't one of those folks who was going to keep running back to my alma mater. Although I was very grateful to have been able to successfully finish my education, I had no desire to return. It was over! I knew moving on from the "troubling memories" as well as the great ones would be my best bet.

This may seem a little odd to most people, but I was thrilled that Sister Miller had offered a room in the church to me, where I could stay until I found something else. And I already had a roommate who was also staying in the church. Her name was "Betty." Later, a teenager named Mary Lou also moved in. "Betty" had lived at the apartment where I lived the previous summer, and although she was as "straight as an arrow" (as compared to my hippie past), we got along. Sister Miller told me I could help with purchasing the food and asked me to help with some other chores. I didn't need to pay rent, but we all knew by then that she had a very limited budget, so it was important for us to conserve water, electric, and other utilities. That type of lifestyle was something that had never occurred to me before, so this type of responsibility was good for me. The next year would be an interesting one for me, one that would confirm the word Sister Miller had spoken over me at our first meeting. Things would certainly not turn out as I thought they would.

In the meantime, I moved into the church and started my job teaching at Shippensburg Junior High School. I don't need to share extensively about my teaching experience, but I will say that I picked up my art major only at the last minute while in college. And although I was creative, Salem College's art program had been built around "Heritage Arts" and a grant from the Disney Corporation, so my knowledge and experience in "fine arts" was shallow at best. I was no Andrew Wyeth, and I knew it! I never looked at this teaching position as a permanent job, but was thrilled to have fun with it while it lasted. The real thrill for me was meeting another relatively new teacher who had been assigned to direct the school play. She didn't know what she was doing, so I agreed to help her with no pay. Together, we were able to put on a successful production of "The Many Loves of Dobie Gillis."

I say all of that to say this—it was a busy few months for all of us. Although Sister Miller had lost her husband, our congregation, now led by the creative genius of Ward Wiser and his family, undertook the project of building a baptismal pool (a dream of both Brother and Sister Miller) under the sanctuary, adjacent to the basement area where we spent a lot of time. Along with that massive project, rooms and a large hallway/library were added, and our goal to get all of this done in time for Conference was reached.

Sister Miller was in and out, attending church meetings here and there, and so was Jim. He travelled a lot with her in those days, and on occasion, I was asked to go along, and did so, even though I was busy. Teaching school, helping here and there at the church, and directing the play kept me occupied. The people working on the project worked like fools all week, and then we would clean up for church on Sunday.

During this time, workers would use a tamping machine. Talk about *dust*! I will never forget one day—we had asked Ward if he was done "tamping" on a Friday night. He said, "yes," and informed us that we could clean up. So "Betty" and I cleaned the whole dusty sanctuary. We were glad it was done for the weekend until we woke up early Saturday morning to a dreaded familiar sound—the tamping machine, and we knew what that meant. I was not a happy camper, and I let everyone know. "Betty" took it well and taught me a good lesson in spite of my terrible attitude.

During these days, we also had some real "fruit loops" staying in the church, and I was one of them! One kid living there had just been released from prison—not jail—*prison* in New York State. His parents' pastor knew Sister Miller, and he was brought to Shippensburg by his parents along with their pastor. He gave the usual sob story most prisoners do—"*I'm innocent!*" But as we all know, it takes living it out for others to realize if he truly had a "jailhouse conversion." His name was Ken, and he was a piece of work; but no one could scare Bishop Miller, not even demons from hell!

Ken had quite a magnanimous, friendly personality, and seemed to genuinely like being at the church. But to be honest, it didn't take us long to realize he was kind of a "spoiled little rich kid." The young girls at the Temple were warned to stay as far away from him as much as we could. I tried, but because he was friendly and the kind of person you could talk to for hours, I found myself in hot water numerous times for sitting and talking with him in the kitchen. To be honest, it seemed like Jim was busy working. Meanwhile, Ken seemed fun enough to hang with, that is, until several weeks later when he threatened to kill several people, including Sister Miller. While talking to her in her apartment, he held on to the back of a chair and shook it violently until every bolt fell out of it and into pieces on the floor! Sister Miller was just thankful he had not chosen to shake her!

It wasn't long before Sister Miller told Ken to move out. She had had enough of his attitude, and he was told to move his guitar and amplifier *out* of the sanctuary as well. That same day, she was downstairs in the basement—in the furnace room, while Ed Schale, Nancy (Lomady) Schale, and I were in the kitchen, when we heard Ken fire up his guitar in utter defiance and begin to play upstairs in the sanctuary. Immediately, Sister Miller came over to the kitchen and said, "Ed, go upstairs, and have him take that guitar and amp out of here right now!"

She wasn't kidding! Nancy and I began to pray; we thought Ken might try to kill Brother Ed. So, we prayed. We listened. We prayed. We listened. And suddenly… silence.

Sister Miller flew out of the furnace room and said, "Did Ed come back down?"

We answered, "Not yet."

That's when we saw two size 6½ high heels go flying across that basement floor, and we heard the infamous "General Custer charge" up the stairs to the sanctuary! We waited and waited. Finally, we heard voices. Then we heard equipment being moved. Next we heard doors bang, and soon, silence again. Then more voices. Then someone stomping across the floor upstairs and a door was slammed shut.

Eventually, Brother Ed descended the steps, seemingly a broken man, with his own story to tell.

We asked, "What happened?" And Ed told his side the best he could, but soon Sister Miller shared her side of the infamous story as well.

When she went up to the sanctuary, she found Ed, cornered by Ken, who was breathing out violence, threatening to crush Ed like a cockroach, if he even *touched* him or his equipment. With one swift move, Sister Miller commanded Ken to remove his equipment! When he refused, she went to the amplifier, grabbed it by the top, drug it to the back of the sanctuary on its wheels, opened the door, and pushed it out onto the porch. She marched back in, grabbed the guitar, took it out, and placed it on the porch as well.

Next, she grabbed Ken by the shirt and proceeded to "escort" him out on the porch along with his banned equipment! After that, she marched back up to Ed and let him know what a wimp he had been and that he should be ashamed of himself for being such a chicken!

Having done her work for the night, she said "good night" to us and closed her door for the day. We have told this story to practically everyone who has come in to our church. Looking back now, it is absolutely hilarious! You couldn't scare Sister Miller! No way! No how!

With regard to my own life, I was trying to be satisfied and happy during those days. Seemingly, it looked like I had everything I wanted. I was engaged to Jim by then. I had a job and nice friends. I loved our church and pretty much got along with Sister Miller, although to be honest about it, at times she kind of scared me. She was way more spiritual than I was, and there was a presence she carried with her that made me nervous, almost like she knew what was going on inside of you and what you were thinking. I know now that was the discernment of spirits which we read about in First Corinthians chapter 12. She really *didn't* know, but the God who she had inside of her knew, and He would orchestrate situations in my own life that would bring about the changes I desperately needed to flush the necessary stuff out of me.

One of the things that would get flushed, and in a hurry, was my relationship with Jim. I had first spent a summer with Jim at Beacon Lodge. We were then together the following summer when I lived in Shippensburg while taking classes. Now I was living in Shippensburg, in the same building with Jim.

This would have been an ideal time to "seal" our friendship and love, but the living arrangement seemed to be doing the opposite. I was getting more miserable all the time. I won't go into the gory details, but our timely breakup came as the result of a basket.

Sister Miller and Jim had gone on another trip together, which as I said, happened a lot. On this particular trip, Jim purchased a basket for me (he knew I *loved* baskets). The problem was, it sat on the counter in the kitchen for two days, and he never told me it was for me.

Finally, Sister Miller said, "Do you like the basket?"

"What basket?" I asked.

She explained that the basket we were both now looking at was for me and that Jim had bought it for me. I was embarrassed, but at the same time, it was a very "telling" situation.

She looked at me and said, "Do you want to live like this?"

I said, "No, I don't."

We were not a good match, and I knew it. Moreover, I was not so desperate that I needed any man. I had found *the* man—His name was Jesus. I knew if I married Jim, it would end anyway, probably not in the divorce court, but in a murder trial (tongue in cheek, folks)! In my mind, it was over.

Conference was in two days, and I hardly saw Jim; but I knew what I had to do. Right in the middle of Conference, I broke our engagement, throwing the ring back at him in a flurry. That was the end. It probably was not the greatest timing on my part, but I felt like Mel Gibson in the movie, "Braveheart"— *freedom*! The crazy part was, Jim hardly reacted. It was just not meant to be.

When the conference ended, my heart was broken, and I had to decide what I wanted to do and what God wanted me to do. In my mind, I had two choices—go home or stay in Shippensburg. After speaking with Sister Miller, and understanding I didn't have a job at that time, I was free to take my own sabbatical. So, I packed my suitcase and went home for some Mom-time. Then I had some choices to make.

In the meantime, it was nice to be home. A lot of my friends there were serving the Lord and fitting into the Christian scene in Mifflin County. To be honest, though, God had already begun to plant me under Sister Miller's ministry, and consequently, the teaching and everything else back home seemed shallow. I am not saying it was, but I believe God allowed me to feel unsatisfied.

One night while sitting in front of our house with Mom and her friend, Don Breon, who would become my step-dad, a thought came to me. *Had I gone to Shippensburg for Jim, or for God?* It didn't take me long to answer that question. Ultimately, it for was the Lord Jesus Christ, and I knew it. I packed my bags, and within a few hours, I was on the road back to zip code 17257, Shippensburg, PA. It would become my permanent address.

Looking back, up until that time, my Christian experience with God and with Sister Miller, my spiritual Mom, had been a "honeymoon." Little did I know, by making the decision to move back to Shippensburg and submit myself under one of the great generals in God's army, I was now about to enter boot camp! It seemed that, overnight, I was on God's hot seat, ready or not, and I was determined that going AWOL was not an option! I had signed up. I *knew* Sister Elvina E. Miller was the real deal, and I wanted to be trained under her, even though I had no idea what that meant!

I guess everyone who signs up for the military has an idea or expectation of how things will probably go once they are in boot camp and then what it will be like when they progress to active service when they are deployed or assigned to a job. I had a somewhat "charismatic— Jesus People Movement" idea of what Christianity was. I was raised a Lutheran and acquired an excellent background in the knowledge of God. I was blessed to be part of a church in my hometown of Yeagertown that had at the helm, a pastor after God's own heart who loved and shepherded me through some tough days in high school and college. I considered anyone who was part of our church under the late Reverend Dean Rupe, privileged. He was a true man of God who became like a father to me, and I know without his singular influence, I would not be serving God today.

However, I came into a better understanding of "being born-again" and actually accepting Jesus Christ as my Savior, asking Him to forgive me of my sins, during the whole revival of the Jesus Movement of the late 1960s and early 1970s. I was the perfect "poster child" for the Jesus Movement. I had been a hippie, and I had come to the end of it. That's a significant realization! I was tired of "plastic" people. Heroin and needles scared me. And when I looked around at the "friends" I had accumulated and the lifestyle I was living, it was a *bummer*—to use a word from that era! Another negative aspect during this time was that all my high school and college friends were moving on. In addition, I felt at odds with my family, and I was. What a disappointment I had become. I felt stupid next to my brother, Rick, and now, I felt like a loser.

When I accepted Jesus as my Lord, I truly loved the experiences I was having in Lewistown. There was Mom Gearhart's Pizza Shop, where I got saved; Praise and Prayer Meetings on Tuesday at the Burnham Brethren Church; Full Gospel Businessmen's Fellowship; and the New Wine Cellar Fellowship out in Dry Valley. I was jumping from meeting to meeting with everyone else. But compared to what I was experiencing in Shippensburg at Deliverance Temple, combined with being taught the foundational truths in

God's Word, everything else seemed empty. I simply believe that God allowed me to feel this way, so that I would take the right steps and get into the right "branch" (for me) of God's military! Dear friends and family of mine, who live out their Christianity in my home area of Mifflin County, are all part of *great* churches there. But for me—God knew I needed Sister Miller, and He had ordered my steps to transfer to that branch of the service. There I would stay and stop jumping here and there! I had signed up!

Earlier, I referred to Sister Elvina E. Miller as a general in God's army. If there can be a higher title, like a ten-star general to bestow upon her, she would be deserving in my mind! Before I had first met her and when I got saved, I had come out of the hippie life and was trying to turn things around. I was trying to dress nicer, and I stopped getting high. But as I began to submit under my pastor, Sister Miller, and allow her to speak into my life, I discovered something unique. You don't have to have been a hippie, wear jeans, smoke pot, do LSD, hitchhike, meditate on your navel, listen to Jefferson Starship, and live immorally to *help* someone who has lived that life. Sister Miller was so far from that! She lived such an innocent life—she didn't even know about the "birds and the bees" when she got married! Plus, according to her own testimonies, she had lived in a home where there was excessive alcohol abuse and wanted no part of it.

Then God sent her to Puerto Rico to do mission work. While there, she received her "on the job" training for our generation, and in my case, specifically for *me*! She held evangelistic meetings in independent churches and in lively Methodist churches all over that island. One day, she was invited to attend, observe, and minister to a large group of hippie converts called the "Catacombes." It was a true move of God in Puerto Rico, and Sister Miller, beautifully dressed, always together, perfectly coiffed, and wearing high heels, found herself right in the thick of a somewhat unsavory group of converts, who met under trees and had not yet discovered why you need to take a bath!

I say all that to say this—nothing I could say or do surprised her, and she *knew* that the hippie movement that I was trying to distance myself from had nothing to do with *how* I dressed. I needed the same simple thing that *every* person needs—an inward change. An inward change will eventually affect the outside of us, and that is what I was about to find out.

God had placed me under a true lady! Looking back again, I cannot believe that she actually put up with hanging out with me. I still reeked of hippie, but God gave her grace. She took it slow but began to sow into my life with truth, God's Word, and a Holy Ghost scrub brush! I've said it before, but truly "those were the days."

As I said earlier, I was in "boot camp," God's boot camp, and my drill sergeant was Sister Miller. In boot camp, you receive training—sometimes, you dig a hole, and then the drill sergeant says, "Fill it back up." That type of task never kills a soldier, but rather, to quote my favorite Kelly Clarkson song, it teaches you that "What doesn't kill you makes you stronger"!

That's the best way to describe how God was working in my life. Sister Miller patiently guided me through some changes in my behavior, morals, and attitude, which would continue to prepare me for what God had in mind for me. To put it bluntly, it didn't always feel good, and I was a bit wimpy, way too sensitive, and was hurt too easily. I definitely needed toughening up!

By the end of the 1970s, a lot had taken place, so I'll make it short and sweet. God had used Sister Miller to help me see that I was a bit of a liar, had problems with unhealthy desires, and suffered with an inferiority complex. The circumstances that brought all this to light aren't worth printing; suffice it to say that during these days, I was tempted to leave the church several times.

Meanwhile, as a lot was happening in my own life, a lot was also happening with my family. My brother, Rick, and his wife, Allison, adopted two kids, Mom was married and happy, and everyone seemed busy. I was totally "dug in" at the church and was probably not doing the best to stay in touch with my family whom I dearly loved. Part of that was my fault, when I allowed thoughts to creep in saying that they didn't want to be around me. I later realized that that was the furthest thing from the truth, especially when I had some *real* heart-to-heart talks with Mom and Aunt Nancy. But I do believe God used my lopsided views, as well as a short period of separation from them, to His advantage.

I was like a plant placed in intense heat, which is fertilized and watered until the roots get strong. That was where I was at that time. I am sure there were zillions of thoughts going through my family's mind, especially since all of this went on at about the time of the "People's Temple" and the Jim Jones thing, as well as the whole PTL Club scandal. I can assure you, we didn't drink any Kool-Aid, and our dogs did not have air-conditioned dog houses. We also saw the writing on the wall concerning the name of our church. While for a time, many non-denominational churches were called temples, after the "People's Temple" horror took place, we chose to distance ourselves by changing our church name. Oasis of Love Church truly fits our aesthetic.

It would have been hard to describe what God was doing in my life to my family. I was having enough trouble understanding it myself. Eventually, God began to peel away what He needed in me; and it took some crazy situations to do so, but it was worth it.

One particular incident always comes to mind about those days, and I have shared it numerous times with the "kids" in our church. I will *never* forget that one day at dinner when I was having a "mini-pity-party" (I was probably hurt over something or didn't get my way), I asked Sister Miller if I could be excused from the table. She excused me, but I had a plan. I was done with this! AWOL or not, I was "out of here." I went to my room and began to pack. So I would not have to face anyone, I planned my escape for late at night. But as I packed, I began to get weak. It was the weirdest thing. As time went on, I could no longer lift my arms to even place one piece of clothing in any of my suitcases. Nevertheless, I continued to try to pack until I was so weak from trying that I just collapsed on the floor in a pool of tears.

I couldn't even leave.

I believe that physical feeling was a supernatural thing that had taken place just for me, just for that moment. God knew, if I walked out that door, that would have been it. His plan for me would have been over.

I shoved that suitcase, half packed, back under my bed so no one would see it. I got up, wiped my eyes, went back to the kitchen, and there she was—my drill sergeant, waiting to see what I was going to do.

"What are you doing, Nancy?" Bishop Miller asked.

I said, "I want to help. I want to be part of this. I don't want my own way. Please forgive my terrible attitude!"

Then she looked at me and simply said, "I forgive you. Now, could you make some finger jello?"

I was so thrilled to have that moment of brokenness. And did I make finger jello! I would have made finger jello until the cows came home! I was back, not just physically, but my heart was also now in it; and that would keep my feet where they belonged, too.

The point here is, I seriously needed a strong hand in my life. I honestly don't think many people realize what happens to kids when they go through a trauma. My father, who I was very close to, died when I was in ninth grade. My mother was very young. My brother was away at college, and there was a major disconnect between my mother and me.

She was in mourning, right when I needed a serious and steady hand in my young life. None of my behavior, rebellion, or insecurity was her fault, but God had Sister Miller ready to take up where my mom was forced to leave off. I know as the years passed, my dear mom finally was able to experience the benefits of what Sister Miller eventually poured into me during those days. I am ever grateful that I got that chance to make finger jello. It was just another day that helped turn my life around.

Dobie Gillis

The Dedication of the Jubilant Hall

My Mother and Don Breon

Bishop on one of her many trips in the
Dominican Republic and Puerto Rico

Aunt Nancy and my mother

Rick, dad, and myself

Chapter Four

"WE ARE FAMILY"—SISTER SLEDGE

Therefore your gates shall be open continually; they shall not be shut day or night....
(Isaiah 60:11 NKJV)

There is a lot I could say about how amazingly Sister Miller handled that period of time, during the 1970s and 80s, in all of our lives. People, and even some ministers, observing from afar, made some assumptions that were uncomplimentary and pretty far from true with regard to what was going on in our church. I would never repeat some of the rumors that had circulated during that time, but they were the furthest things from reality that you could possibly imagine. If you truly *knew* Sister Miller and the standard of righteousness she upheld, you could have *never* believed what was "going around" out there. It reminded me of those who would call our church a cult, but who had never darkened the door to actually have gathered any evidence to the contrary. That was obviously the work of the enemy who comes to steal, divide, and destroy.

During that period of time, there was a large group of young college students living on the premises, and there were many others who didn't live here, but were around so much that you could say they almost did live here. There was a continuous in and out, late nights, and many worship services out on our lawn. Combined with all the activity around the Temple, it wasn't difficult to believe that a "commune" had formed on South Washington Street. But it had not.

Let me be the one to assure you, because I lived through it. Nothing unholy, uncivilized, or illegal was going on, in or around our church, nor has it ever. Actually, Bishop Miller was doing her best to whip another branch of God's army together to fight all that stuff!

Still, there were many who talked, and I guess they had their reasons.

First of all, Sister Miller already had a reputation in our town. By reputation, I mean this—when she and Brother Miller initially built our church back in 1951-52, a lot of people from many local churches flocked to her meetings.

Strike one!

Add to that the fact that Sister Miller—a woman—as I shared earlier, seemed to be the dominant minister.

Strike two!

Also, during those early times, Sister Miller travelled to Cuba over the course of several years. When she, along with Brother Miller came home one time, they experienced a huge church split, which occurred because the Millers stood their ground against sin. That stand would flush three-quarters of the people out of the church. Boy, did the rumors fly!

Strike three!

The rumors that flew should have impacted the people who left; they were the offenders. But because those people were part of the church *during* and *while* they were participating in immoral activity, those rumors stuck to our church and to Sister Miller.

It's hard to live that stuff down, but the Millers were all the more determined to live life beyond that split. They knew God had promised them a new day, and they were living stellar and impeccable Christian lives.

Like I said, our church and Sister Miller already had a reputation. In my observation, disgruntled people who leave churches aren't always the most reliable for spewing out facts about their former church. What sometimes comes out of their mouths is according to "their view," which is often negative, and which usually spreads fast. There's a song sung by Susan Ashton, which says, "It started as a whisper, spread into a rumor, turned into lies." And that's about how it goes! Have you ever noticed that people would rather listen to the negative stuff than the good?

At the time our gang of new believers showed up at Sister Miller's door, she had already endured a major church split, followed by 13 lonely years waiting for the congregation to arrive that God had promised her. When we began to trickle in the door, she didn't care what or who God gave her! After those 13 long years, she just wanted to share Jesus, how good He is, and all the glorious things she had seen in His Word with *anyone*!

Later in years, she told us she would lay hands on the phone and *pray* that it would just *ring*! But it didn't. I'm embarrassed to admit this today, but there are times that I get half irritated with the constant ringing of that phone. Then I am reminded about her prayer and that silences me pretty quickly!

Sister Miller didn't care *who* God brought for her to minister to; consequently, we hosted a huge influx of some really unusual characters who came to the doors of Deliverance Temple for help. To any common observer, they looked and acted like your basic everyday generalization of a criminal, a druggie, or a hippie. But to Sister Miller, they were souls that needed to be saved, and she would go into the highways and the byways to do whatever it took to compel any of them to come in.

Along with that type of new believer, Sister Miller also had an influx from the campus ministry, many who knew far more than she did, or so they thought. After all, they had been saved for three months! I remember one incident when Nancy Schale, who is now one of our pastors, asked someone if they thought Sister Miller was saved.

Is Sister Miller saved?

My response today is, if she's not saved, nobody is! Back then, though, I probably would have wondered the same thing. I think you know what I'm saying—we were the epitome of "spiritual sputniks."

Don't forget, Sister Miller was juggling these circumstances almost single-handedly. At one time, there were about 25 of us living in the building. One whole summer, I lived in an entranceway. No worries, we didn't use that door anymore, so I did have privacy.

It was now the late 1970s. With a gang of "kids" in their early and mid-twenties, some teenagers here and there, a few families, and three or four older folks, our church was truly a motley crew! Sister Miller, however, was doing her utmost to steer the ship. She did everything to keep on top of anything that could potentially "go wrong" and tried to keep us totally occupied 100 percent of the time. She didn't want us to have any time to get into trouble, but trouble was my middle name.

I can now only imagine how her family felt.

Brother and Sister Miller had two children, Myrna and Lyle. Myrna lived a few hours away; Lyle lived in Arizona. Sister Miller was inundated with her care for us and the continual drain it must have been to have full responsibility for a whole "nursery" full of new Christian babies! Just picture it this way—when one would start screaming, she would have to grab a bottle and feed him. Then another one would scream because he had made a mess. Then another would drop his toy. Another needed to sleep. Then it would start all over again. It just never ended! This may explain why she didn't have that much time to travel to every family event. Oh, she wanted to, but she was so pleased to *finally* have a decent-sized congregation to minister to. It must have been *thrilling*, no matter how we looked.

At this point, I need to back-track a little. In 1974, Brother and Sister Miller celebrated their 40th wedding anniversary. Our "thoughtful" gang at the church surprised them with a huge party for the happy event.

The only problem was, we never invited anyone from their family.

Now, anyone could understand why there may have been some hard feelings down the road. I know today, all is forgiven, but our actions, or neglect to act, didn't contribute to "good vibrations" during that interesting period of time.

For a good many years, Brother and Sister Miller were almost solely responsible for the upkeep of the church. I am not saying there was no one else in the church who helped, but there was a *large* building and some grounds to maintain… and the Millers lived with and believed in excellence for God. They didn't have a home at that time, so they cared for God's house even better than most people care for their own homes. During the "alone" years at the church, those 13 long years, I am sure there were limited finances and manpower to provide the necessary upkeep. General daily maintenance was probably all they could *handle* with their small congregation and even smaller budget. So, imagine how Sister Miller felt when she had a few extra hands. She had to be *thrilled*!

Sister Miller was also full of ideas, plus, as I already shared, she felt the push to keep us busy, and she was an expert at it! We cleaned the church. And we sat in Bible Studies that lasted for hours. Then, she got inspired to plant a garden (to help feed *us*)! She had already established a radio show, so she worked on training us to assist, but not take her place. We weren't ready for that; she was a consummate professional!

Things that had not been painted for years, we painted, and by the late 1970s, early 1980s, we were adding on. Eventually, we bought additional land, built two buildings, and inhabited those buildings as well. We began to print a monthly newsletter/magazine. And we formed a singing group that we thought was "off the chain," but frankly sounded pretty terrible. But we loved to sing, and that's all that mattered.

There was a lot going on. Countless students and young people moved in and out, joined up, then went AWOL. But through all this time, a nucleus of people stayed and received what God wanted to impart to them through this wonderful saint, Sister Miller, and she was a good teacher. She was concerned about mind, body, and soul, and seemed to have an uncanny ability to balance all three. So spiritual, so truly holy, yet she was a blast to be around. Plus, she always looked fabulous, and she used her physical assets to the best of her ability. You were proud to go anywhere with her; she made *you* look good!

Not surprisingly, I was naturally drawn to her, and as time went on, we became almost inseparable. I loved her as if she were my mom, and she grew to love me, caring for me through several almost disastrous relationships. She may have known I would not marry, but she never discouraged me and always wanted me to be happy. In time, however, I realized that my choice of men was, well, a disaster waiting to happen.

Bishop Miller and I spent so much time together over the years that she actually started to talk like me. Unfortunately for her, I constantly repeated several phrases that were carried over from my hippie days. I could hardly believe when these words and phrases suddenly became part of her everyday lingo! She would say, "What a riot!" "We're goin' on a thunder run," "This place is a circus!" or some other Nancy-ism that had crept into her vocabulary. It was proof that we were practically inseparable! I never could get her to say "groovy" or "far out," though. (I still hold on to those for myself!)

Back to my point—Bishop Miller, as she is now called, knew she had to go easy on me. Keep in mind, I was "allergic" to work. I had not done much of what you would call "work" up until that point in my life, and she probably realized it. As a result, it seemed as though I was always the one she asked to drive her here, and there, and everywhere, while other people weeded and planted. So, did I ever do gardening, painting, and good old-fashioned work? Definitely, I did my fair share, although I can't say I wasn't happy whenever she had something else for me to do. (I haven't mentioned it, but by then, Jim had flown the coop, and that was fine with me!) I had a VW bug, a red one, and speaking of "flying," that car flew all over the landscape. It seemed that shopping always became a part of our adventures. And if you know me, that actually explains a lot!

It is hard to describe how intense these days were at our church. It is one of those "you had to be there" times. It may be hard to understand, but God is able by His Word and power to examine us inside out. He is like the best MRI machine on the planet to find out what ails us; and He uses His ministers, those who are blessed with discernment, to read our "x-ray" and tell us what's going on. At other times, He will use circumstances to bring us to the end of ourselves, so that we look to Him.

As time goes on, there is one thing with regard to physical illness that always "blows my mind." We get sick, and then we run to the doctor. And if he tells us to drink turpentine and gargle with dish soap ten times a day, some folks will do it, just because the doctor says to do it. Because that doctor has been trained in the medical field, we think we should listen to him or her. Then there is the minister, the one who has faithfully served God for years studied His Word, and lives a life to be admired and emulated. But let that minister diagnose your spiritual problem, and people are *out the door*!

I have to say, there were some tough days, tough words, and tough times that I endured as I allowed God to do surgery on me through Dr. Miller and the Holy Spirit. I don't know of any *actual* surgery that is fun or comfortable to recover from, do you? I often tried to run away from "the knife," but thankfully, God's grace prevailed and I stuck it out. Soon, I was not nervous around Bishop Miller any longer. She began to trust me; I began to trust me. And that thing, which drove me in my earlier years to a life of drugs, drink, dishonesty, and depravity, was defeated in my life. That "thing" is called sin, and we all deal with it!

How do you fill a hole in your being that is occupied with all kind of stuff not worth living for? There's only one thing, one Person, who will ever satisfy—Jesus. When I look around, speaking from my role as a pastor, I see several kinds of Christians today, two of which I'll address here. First, there are those Christians who teeter-totter on the verge of sin. They hang together like highschool kids, and you can't tell them anything because they never give you the opportunity. They live a very selfish, immature Christianity and are often about to topple over the edge. Plus, can I add, that most of them do not answer to any real mature authority over them.

Then, there's another kind of believer—the ones who don't avoid leadership. They stay involved and are givers of their time and money. I can speak into their lives, and I do. The problem is, sometimes these Christians grow up in church—protected. Then they get a taste of "the things of this world," and they start to gravitate toward them. The devil's mission is to take us down and pull us away. It usually happens slow and easy through a compromise of the values we never thought we would ever break. But then God brings us to a fellowship of believers, under a leader where we can develop strong roots and *grow.* If we allow God that growing season, He can pour on the fertilizer, along with the weed killers, and destroy the stuff that can entangle and eventually destroy us.

Why do I share this? I had plenty of opportunities to bolt and go AWOL—"make like a tree and leave," "exit, stage left". But an honest hunger for God tugged at my heart. I truly wanted to serve God, and nothing was going to stop me. I thank God every day for that strong, firm, truth-telling, spiritual Mom whom God placed over me, to reel me in. Sister Miller was like an Army drill sergeant for me, and just like in the Army, I had nowhere to run, nowhere to hide.

I wished we would have kept a diary during the late 1970s and very early 1980s. Most folks would never believe the influx of people that Sister Miller endured. Yes, endured! Let me describe just one of those saints. I will leave out his full name to protect the innocent.

Let's talk about "Bruce." Bruce came to Sister Miller from Franklin County Prison. He was originally from Colorado and was intelligent, good-looking, personable, *and* a felon. We took him in at the request of the prison chaplain, and he lived in the same building with a whole gang of girls—me included. It didn't take long to realize that Bruce had a way with words and a way with just about everything. Soon, he had gained Sister Miller's trust and was responsible for night watch, cooking, and was in charge of the garden. He occasionally had a few minor run-ins with Sister Miller and some of the guys, but the thing that eventually sparked our concern was that he refused to be baptized. He always had a reason why he couldn't do so and kept saying he just wasn't ready. Yet clearly, God's Word says that we need to believe and be baptized to be saved: *"He who believes and is baptized will be saved; but he who does not believe will be condemned"* (Mark 16:16 NKJV).

It wasn't long before Bruce had "conveniently" talked Sister Miller into going organic by proposing that we buy about 50,000 praying mantises to control the bugs in our one-acre garden. He also had us sifting soil. Grrrr… talk about a flesh-and-back killer! One fine day, a police car rolled onto the property, and minutes later, Bruce was in the cruiser taking a ride to the station to answer some questions. After a few hours, the police returned to tell us that Bruce was behind bars—he was wanted in Colorado for indecent exposure and incest. Talk about God's protection, mercy, and grace as we escaped any incident while he was with us.

But then there were the praying mantises.

Quickly, Mary Lou, our treasurer, ran to retrieve the mail bag, hoping it was still on our premises. Thankfully, she found the bag, and there, lying at the bottom of that bag was the order form and the check, all sealed in an envelope, *almost* on its way to Burpee's. Most of us, if not everyone, was glad to tear that order in half and go back to our "chemical warfare" on the bugs!

Our famous singing group, late 70's early 80's

One of the articles that appeared in the news in the 1950's

The Oasis of Love Church, God's Promises are forever!

Myrna and Bursie

Lyle and Cris

The LOVE HUB

The Utility Building

My Spiritual Mom

Mary Lou Swartz,
our long time treasurer

Chapter Five

BUILDING A CHURCH, PIECE BY PIECE

The glory of Lebanon shall come to you, the cypress, the pine, and the box tree together, to beautify the place of My sanctuary; and I will make the place of My feet glorious.
(Isaiah 60:13 NKJV)

An even stronger nucleus of believers had bonded together in our church during the 1980s and were the pillars God would use to guide our church into the next phase of growth. Sister Miller was traveling extensively; after all, she was called to do so. I know that she likewise loved all of her opportunities at our home church, to build it up through the laying down of foundational truths. This included the catechism "Understanding God" by Rev. Patricia Beall Gruits. Without a doubt, though, she loved the worldwide opportunities she experienced as she traveled and preached the Gospel. During that time in her life, she did a lot of it alone. Meanwhile, in between her travels, she was here with us, continuing to nourish and care for the plants (us), who were being cultivated in our "greenhouse," our church.

Sister Miller was gifted with an unusual revelation of God's Word. If you were not around or did not benefit from her teaching, you may not understand this statement, or perhaps, you may take it the wrong way. But actually, Sister Miller was ahead of her time. She danced in church before it was cool, and she led us to form a dance troupe, years before anyone else did. She adapted to rock-and-roll and newly birthed spiritual songs, because she wrote so many herself, long before you heard of Chris Tomlin and other worship leaders. I don't say this to discredit any of those blessed and honorable worship leaders; I simply wish to emphasize that while Sister Miller didn't believe in contemporary worship per se, she believed in *worship*—as the natural and spiritual progression of the unveiling of God's Word, resulting from the teaching of presently revealed truth.

For this reason I will not be negligent to remind you always of these things, though you know and are established in the present truth (2 Peter 1:12 NKJV).

Present truth would produce songs birthed out of that experience. It only stands to reason that new music would come forth out of new generations of believers, and God began to give all of us new worship songs. These songs were birthed out of our experience with Jesus and the teaching of His Word. For several years, I seemed to get a song for every Conference, and I believe God expected nothing less.

...For everyone to whom much is given, from him much will be required; and to whom much has been committed, of him they will ask the more (Luke 12:48 NKJV).

Our worship services were unique. Sister Miller started out playing the organ, and several people shared duties on the piano. Ed Schale played the guitar, and it wasn't long until other guitar players, some experienced, and others new, began to play. At one time during that period, there were ten people playing the guitar! Others played flute, clarinet, saxophone, piccolo; it was pretty cool. It was the move of the Spirit in those days. No one was really that good, but we played. We had drummers come and go, just like the pianists; but again, a hunger and a nucleus of skilled musicians began to blossom. This would be the core group who would lead us into the future.

I have to say, looking back, I loved Sister Miller's method. She did not believe musicians or singers were special or stars. Did you get that? Music was *not* the most important part of the service. Oh, it's important, but according to God's Word, it is to pave the way for the preaching of the Word.

The singers went before, the players on instruments followed after; among them were the maidens playing timbrels (Psalm 68:25 NKJV). Because musicians weren't elite, Sister Miller required that they be a part of the regular Levitical service in the Lord's house. The Levites were called out to serve the tabernacle and all of its workings in the Old Testament. Today, that equates to each of us having a responsibility and being involved in the care and upkeep of the Lord's house, our church.

If the only service you perform is to walk in and play your instrument on Sunday, you have missed the point. Anyone who attends and is fed at a local church, is responsible to give back. It would be similar to going out to dinner, sitting down to eat, having the staff wait on you, serve you, and cook for you. Then you eat and get up to leave without paying the bill. How sad and how selfish. Yet we do that in church all the time. We walk into a clean building, having only come with our music, while the ministers have already sought God and prepared the Word to serve us. We sit down, pay our tithes (maybe we think that's enough), get up, and leave. That cash should never be to care for the basic needs of a church building when there are able bodies available to complete those tasks as volunteers. That's giving back! Psalm 110:3 NKJV says, *"Your people shall be volunteers in the day of Your power; in the beauties of holiness, from the womb of the morning, You have the dew of Your youth."* In other words, why use the dew of youth to waste it on unfruitful stuff. Give to God's house while you have the strength to do so!

Sister Miller also taught us that if we wanted to be up front, leading or playing, our life had to be right. While God was busy building a nucleus, shining His searchlight on our lives through Sister Miller and His Word, there were occasions when musicians would be asked to take a break and not play their instrument for a period of time. I can actually remember times when *no one* played an instrument, except Sister Miller. Thank God for soundtrack tapes, which filled in when folks were taking a "time out." At that point, those folks knew they were struggling with an area in their lives, and they willingly walked away from leading worship in God's house until they were cleared up or cleaned up on the inside. We still believe that.

Recently, a young person in our church was struggling with alcohol abuse. He knew, and I knew, that he had no place leading worship. Gradually, he is being restored. Keep in mind, we bring a curse to that holy position of leading worship when we are involved in sin. Standing as God's minister is a high calling, one that Sister Miller held honorably. She expected from us only what she was also willing to do, and that is how it should be.

That's why hirelings don't always work. I am thankful for Bishop Miller's teaching. We have only ever "hired" one musician. I can still hear her say, "Raise up your own, then you know what you are getting." Any time we have attempted to "bring someone in" to do something in ministry that should be "home-grown," it has not worked.

Psalm 37:16 says, *"A little that a righteous man has is better than the riches of many wicked"* (NKJV). Believe me, I know hiring someone is not wrong, but I am baffled that we aren't more attentive to God's Word concerning these things. In David's Tabernacle, which was *known,* and still known, for its worship, they played the instruments David built! Talk about raising up your own. Figuratively, that is a great illustration. You don't have instruments? Make them yourself!

If you teach and train those who will lead, sing, and teach others, you know who they are and what "stuff" they are made from. It is so important to know *how* a person lives behind closed doors, so that you also know that the holiness they "put on" is a true holiness within their hearts and lives. If you take a look at the exciting passages that describe the times of worship in David's Tabernacle, you see all manner of families being brought up to worship and serve together. Sister Miller held to that! She believed you had to be holy to stand up before people and lead them into the holy place of God's presence in worship, and she believed you should raise up your leaders from within the church. It's a scripturally sound teaching.

Story time again. Sister Miller also traveled a lot, back and forth to New York City, to minister. She truly fit in with all those lovely Italian believers in NYC. She was a dynamic, intelligent, and attractive woman and really had the ability to draw people from many different backgrounds and professions. We don't fully remember how all this went down, but at one point, a professional musician from Long Island came to Shippensburg with his new bride to take over as the head of our music ministry. We'll call him "Fred." Contrary to what Bishop Miller herself believed, she gave "Fred" full reign over our choir, musicians, and worship. He was immediately "elevated," received an income, and was given a place to live. It didn't take long for us to see the writing on the wall—this was not going to work. While "Fred" was definitely talented, it was evident that his spirit was unruly, and he treated many of us like doormats. Don't misunderstand me, Sister Miller required that he be a part of our classes and teaching; but after a time, he even began to boss her around. Not good.

Certainly, our music sounded *great*, but was it worth it? In time, I believe "Fred" began to realize that this wasn't just some "gig" he had signed a contract for, and he moved back to Long Island. Right after he left, the near meltdown took place at the nuclear power plant on Three Mile Island, and "Fred" told his associates in NYC that God had told he and his wife to leave to avoid the disaster. I beg to differ. I do believe God told him to leave—to avoid a greater problem here in our church. With his non-compliant, arrogant ways, he would have destroyed many young believers. Now *that* would have been a nuclear meltdown and disaster!

After this experience together, Sister Miller and each of us learned a deep and important lesson. Never again!

At another time, a group of us were preparing for a trip to NYC to be with Sister Miller while she ministered at a church in Queens. Right before we left, though, one of the young men was involved in a situation involving alcohol, and his wife felt he should not be a part of the trip. Sister Miller agreed and always made sure she took clean vessels to be used. She would have never risked playing with fire on an important ministry trip. We may have had a few cracks, but at least we were pretty well cleaned up.

Don't misunderstand me here. As I shared, we were not perfect. Bishop Miller simply taught how ministers should conduct themselves and asked us to uphold a standard. She didn't want us, down the road, to experience what goes on sometimes today—a minister gets caught in an affair, but in one month he or she is back in the pulpit. She didn't believe in that kind of ministry. Yet she was compassionate and firm on forgiveness. She readily acknowledged repentance, and she was always the first one to forgive, just like Jesus would have done.

One of my all-time favorite stories that has to do with alcohol and forgiveness occurred when I lived in a home full of single ladies on Walnut Street. It was the mid-80s, and we all were employed while also "dug-in" at our church. It just so happened, though, that my roommate was having an on-and-off battle with alcohol. She would do well for a while, and then "fall off the wagon," as they say.

One Saturday night, I was at the church, and I had just dutifully, like Martha, prepared the lunch for Sunday. (I considered myself so holy.) Afterward, I returned to our home on Walnut Street to find my roommate passed out on her bed with a fifth of vodka next to her bed, half gone, and another empty bottle turned on its side halfway under the bed. I was indignant! What was I going to do with her?

I called the church. In those days, most of the time, Sister Miller answered the phone, and I explained my dilemma.

With no comment about my "self-righteous" rant, she said, "Nancy, put the empty bottle in a garbage bag. Dump what's left of the fifth down the drain and put it with the other bottle in the bag. You can throw that in the garbage tomorrow."

I said, "What should I do about 'so and so'?"

Her loving reply was, "Nancy, just go to bed. I'll worry about her tomorrow." And with that she hung up.

Most likely, after we ended our conversation, she walked the floor in intercession for this child of God. The next day, before I was awake and before church began, my roommate had made her way to Sister Miller. When I went to the church to take breakfast to Sister Miller, there was my roommate, weeping on her knees in front of her pastor, who was lovingly holding her head in her hands as she prayed for her. Thankfully, I was welcome to join, and we all sought God there in that room, which has seen many tears and bore many bended knees over time. Countless times, I am sure the knees it bore were Bishop Miller's.

It may sound extreme, but Sister Miller truly lived the Word. She was constantly on a mission assignment from God, and she required that everyone else be "ready for ministry." A reasonable person would never allow someone with the measles to go with a doctor to visit children in the hospital. Yet talented people who have spiritual "measles" stand up and sing in choirs, lead worship, and play instruments all the time. That's crazy! It wasn't good enough just to be talented; Sister Miller wanted our talents circumcised and set apart for God. She wanted us to be able to stand in the holy place before God and serve as His vessel, one which He could pour through.

Speaking of forgiveness, I will *never* forget one time when Sister Miller and I had a major clash in her living room. For the life of me, I cannot remember what it was about, but I was arguing with her about something. I probably didn't like some advice I was given and got snippy. And if any of you are like me and have gotten snippy, you probably have felt rotten, especially if you were snippy to someone you loved. Finally, I admitted that I was wrong. After I apologized, I left her room that evening with my tail between my legs and my lip hanging on the ground.

The next morning, as I did every Sunday morning, I prepared coffee and breakfast for Bishop Miller and had to ascend that staircase and face her once again. I had been trying to think of someone who could take my place, because I didn't feel worthy enough to clean up the garbage and after I had been so disrespectful to her. But I went, and as I knocked on the door and heard that familiar "Come in," I was greeted with a bright and delightful smile, and then a "thank you." She asked me what the weather was like; I answered her and then turned to leave. When I was almost out the door, she said, "Nancy, I'm sorry to ask you this so late… do you mind leading worship this morning?"

Me? Scum of the earth. *Me?* Worthless piece of trash. Yes, me. Forgiven, imperfect believer, me. She obviously had forgotten all about our encounter, or better yet, she truly did forgive my blunder. There was no sign that she held anything against me. Thank you, Lord, for a true leader, a true mother in Zion, a true friend.

I thank God for these standards. Because of them, I can look at our ministers and musicians and know that they can be trusted. They have walked through the dealings of God, the fire of His Holy Spirit, and allowed the chaff to be burned. It's not an easy process, but it is a process that must take place in our lives. If it doesn't take place or you run out the door, dragging your family or friends with you at the earliest sign of "heat" from that fire, you'll fit somewhere, but you won't fit in a church that believes in the authority of God and His leaders.

I always pray, "Lord, please don't let us be any other way, or all those years of sacrifice, which Sister and Brother Miller walked through, will go down the tubes, and fast!" I know times change, but God's Word does not. I pray we always have a nucleus within our church that upholds these truths of righteousness.

Sister Miller also cautioned us that there will always be those who come in and go out, who never really see the vision of what God is doing. However, our norm should be that when people come in, they are gradually drawn into more truth, more responsibility, more reliability, and a greater dependability. That's how you grow in the faith. But when saints do start to withdraw, they are most likely getting cold or have missed the mark on why we commit to a church body. In any case, it is to be a gradual building process. I eventually saw that Sister Miller never got overly "shook up" when people left our church. While most of the time I was in pieces over it, she barely batted an eye. She cared, *but* she knew if God was building and had established our church, no man would be able to take it down. It was His to worry about, not ours! Our responsibility was to keep preaching the truth, live right, and spread the Gospel. And God would have His way.

Bishop Miller teaching the catechism "Understanding God"

Services in the 1980's

Sister Miller with kids

Bishop Miller and I ministering together

Chapter Six

IN THE WORLD BUT NOT OF THE WORLD

…ye shall be witnesses unto Me both in Jerusalem, and in all Judaea, and in Samaria,
and unto the uttermost part of the earth.
(Acts 1:8 KJV)

If I had time to share every detail of the comings and goings that took place at our church, "the books could not contain it." When those of us who have been at our church for a while begin to reminisce, it can get pretty crazy. A lot of tears! A lot of laughs! We have gone through some amazing times together, and we often say, "We should write a book, but no one would believe it!"

As I considered where I should head next in this literary journey, I knew it was important to share how Bishop Miller began to direct us with regard to personal involvement in our community. Looking back, I can see that the Millers always believed in "being a part of where you lived," and "not hiding in a cave." Before they found their way to Shippensburg, Brother and Sister Miller had a legacy of involvement in politics, encouraging people to register to vote and generally exercise their freedoms. After all, before the story of this book began, they had lived for a time in Cuba, establishing a church there, but were forced to leave due to the rise and takeover by Castro and the Communist Party. When you've witnessed a takeover, firsthand, of an evil revolution, it's understandable that you would be on the lookout for any pending signs of the same happening within your own country.

Brother and Sister Miller got involved in politics as soon as they were back in the States, participating in rallies and standing strong for conservative values in the USA. They hosted meetings and invited various speakers to town. And then, Sister Miller turned her radio broadcast into a political one. There were several voices proclaiming those values at that time, and she was one of them along with her personal friend, the famous late Rev. Dr. Carl McIntyre. Google him—you'll see what I mean.

As the church became Sister Miller's greater priority, she turned her broadcast once again to a Gospel message broadcast. But, she still took the opportunity to encourage us to open our eyes to the political landscape in our country. She pointed out when things were slowly taking on that scary, liberal philosophy that she had likewise witnessed in Cuba, which made a way for the socialism and the communism that all but destroyed a once pristine and beautiful place.

We held political meetings, and she advised us to think for ourselves on a godly level. Subsequently, when we did so, I believe her instruction gave us extra "antennas" and our own "radar" with which we learned how our nation could be destroyed in just a few generations. We also learned that we can fight back through our freedom of speech and our vote.

When I arrived on the scene in Shippensburg, I came with an American flag sewn on my sleeping bag. I'm not sure what possessed me to do that; I guess I was creating my own little Woodstock world. Pastor Ed had a similar mind-set as he approached the Millers, asking to use their duplicating machine in order to print posters to be used for a Vietnam War protest on the college campus. Talk about Sister Miller taking advantage of a "teaching moment." Even so, these were the people she had to work with, and she took on the challenge.

She also taught us that there's a world out there of which you can influence but only if you are part of it. And so it began. Members of our church ran for office and won, ran for school board and won, joined political parties and are still vital parts of that scene today. It was her influence that inspired us to begin to volunteer in the community and to open the doors of our church in an even greater way to the community. We served community banquets and volunteered for community events. We hosted blood drives, garden tours, and church tours. On top of that, we became a vital part of a campaign to close a massage parlor ("gentleman's club"), which involved picketing for years. Through that service alone, we gained many friends in the community, as we supported each other in that effort. Today, that awful place is closed. (And as an aside, I don't know of one "gentleman" who frequents those places.)

This sense of active volunteerism is a pillar that our church has been built on, and continues to be what makes us tick on a level which Bishop Miller always believed was what *every* church should strive for. The church should be the main spiritual and volunteer organization in every community. Unfortunately, we as a nation have moved away from this task, and I think it is because the Church has somewhat shirked her responsibility, in general, to be Jesus' hands on the earth. Sister Miller didn't worry about what everyone was doing around us; she was concerned with how *we* were obeying Jesus' commands.

In addition, Bishop Miller was always a parade person. And because of her involvement in multiple parades, guess what? The church became involved in parades! If there was a parade, we were in it. Christmas parades, fair parades, town anniversary parades, Halloween parades, parades in Chambersburg… you name it, we were there! Parades are good for three reasons: you "champion" your cause, you get your name out there, and your self-confidence increases. When Bishop Miller was available, she *loved* participating on a float, or in a car, or truck, waving away… throwing candy…throwing tracts.

Along with being *in* the parade, Sister Miller taught us *how* to be in the parade. As her flock, we were not permitted to slap some float together any old way. It had to be the very best float. It would have moving parts, music, costumes. Every time we did something, we had to do it *right;* if we couldn't do it right, we wouldn't do it at all. That's just the way Sister Miller rolled, and that's the way she taught us to roll.

I remember when one of our pastors was given the opportunity to become a police officer. He is now retired, and his story soundly illustrates Sister Miller's unwavering sense of duty to her flock and concern for the community. Before Pastor Jerome Kater agreed to step into the schooling that he would need to become an officer on the university campus, he sought Sister Miller's counsel. I remember being within a few feet of her stern, loving instructions to Jerome as she spoke to him about authority and the abuse of authority. She seriously offered some important words that he says shaped his attitude and the way he conducted his career and still lives his life.

I know I have already shared this part, but I'd like to say it again—Sister Miller's philosophy of "being in the world, but not of the world" echoed Jesus' words to us, to be "the light of the world," "the salt of the earth," and "a city on a hill." How can this world change without the influence of the Body of Christ and what God has done in our lives? That's our job. Remember the acronym—WWJD?—What Would Jesus Do? This question then becomes not just a catch phrase, but the manner in which we conduct our lives in whatever position we find ourselves. We were taught, "Be the change," before it was found written on any t-shirts. The Church of the Lord Jesus Christ should be the arms and hands of Jesus reaching out to a world which may not understand who He is. We shouldn't just be helping our "own"; we should be ready to seek out the stranger, for we may be the only Jesus they ever meet.

Patriotic Parade

One of the MANY Parades

Chapter Seven

F.F.F.—FOOD, FUN, AND FELLOWSHIP

Use hospitality one to another without grudging.
(1 Peter 4:9 KJV)

The biblical truth of reaching out and caring for others with clothing, housing, and feeding people was "for-real" stuff to Sister Miller, and embracing that truth was passed on to us. As I shared earlier, Bishop Miller used food—cooking it, sharing it, and giving it away—as a way to reach out to many, including all of us. The indelible impression that one special dinner Bishop Miller arranged for me is a constant personal reminder of how small gestures can reach beyond a person's stomach and into his or her soul. This manner of ministry would be another way that Sister Miller incorporated a family atmosphere and a "feel" for our church that would "set us apart" yet would cause others to misunderstand the inner workings of our church at times.

An old adage, "The way to a man's heart is through his stomach," is pretty true. But allow me to add that *everyone* needs to eat, and most of us rather enjoy it! Sister Miller came from Italian descent and a family who fully enjoyed the glories of homemade sauce, homemade pasta…well…homemade everything. Add to that the influence of Brother Miller's Pennsylvania German-Dutch heritage, and we enjoyed another whole gamut of culinary yummies that had invaded Sister Miller's cooking and kitchen knowledge. She was a smart lady and knew college students—*everyone* is made up of, not just soul and spirit, but *body* as well. Herein you have the perfect outreach combination: Feed the body and feed the soul. With Sister Miller, you knew both would receive some gourmet offerings!

Because the Millers lived *in* the church, they ate *in* the church; and because a gang of people were always hanging out *at* the church, we either got invited, invited ourselves, or somehow managed to be around during meal times. I am sure most of the time, our presence put a real "wrench" into Sister and Brother Miller's romantic dinner plans (while he lived), but in their minds, outreach, especially to a needy generation, was important.

Now the question has to be asked—how do you feed hungry college students when you barely have enough money to keep the doors of the church open? Two words: pasta and garden! Sister Miller was Italian, and Italians make spaghetti sauce from scratch. To make sauce, you need tomatoes, tomatoes, and more tomatoes. You need onions, fresh parsley, fresh basil, fresh garlic, and just about any kind of meat you can rustle up. Whether Sister and Brother Miller had much gardening experience, I'll never really know, but one thing was for sure, they looked like they knew what they were doing.

Planting a garden Sister Miller-style became a work of art by the time it was done; and in the meantime, she harnessed the spirit, vigor, and strength of our youthful enthusiasm and put us to work. We measured out the land, measured each aisle, measured the distances between each planting, and for several years, planted enough for the "Russian Army." It's possible to say that one person hated that garden so much that it contributed to their demise in our church. But I am happy to say that that person is now back and rejoicing that we no longer plant a half-acre garden each summer.

On a personal level, I have to admit that I was no fan of gardening, but looking back, I am thankful for every ounce of obedience I experienced getting behind that vision, keeping my mouth shut, and allowing that challenge to work a good work in me. I learned to make spaghetti sauce, can, freeze, cook all those delicious fresh vegetables, and grew to love lettuce sandwiches (yes, you heard me right), tomato sandwiches, and BLT's with bacon bits (not real bacon, which was too expensive). It was food, and with the advent and continuance of the garden, we had the resources to feed people. I believe while it lasted, it was a tremendous training tool. While I despised some of those days, today I am the *main* proponent to using every living vegetable and fruit on the planet during its time "in season." I love cooking from scratch, and we continue to train each coming generation the values of cooking, serving, and hospitality.

Today, while we no longer plant that *huge* garden, we have not ceased to be frugal. First of all, we have joined hands with Second Harvest, a Food Bank network, where many times we are blessed to be the beneficiaries of cases and cases of tomatoes and many other fruits and vegetables. When the food bank in Harrisburg has an excess, they call us, because they know we will can, freeze, or make some type of use of the fresh vegetables that many other agencies walk away from because they do not have the staff available to preserve vegetables. All those years of vegetable raising and harvesting have really taught us the value of "waste not, want not," and has saved us a lot of money over the years.

It's taken me a while to get to this part of the chapter, but here goes. I hope you have been able to glean that our church was and *is* like a big house. Actually, it's like a big *home*! There is a difference. A house is a building; a home is an atmosphere. In today's world, there is a lot of emphasis placed on aesthetics. You go to a good restaurant for two reasons—the food and the atmosphere. I actually think that food and atmosphere should be prerequisites for a church as well. Sister Miller knew how to create an atmosphere, and she never shied away from teaching us how important that was to her. Our church had and continues to have a definite family atmosphere.

Again, Sister Miller was a fantastic cook. She was creative and did not need a recipe, but she understood that not everyone had that same gift. For some, it had to be developed. Early on, she did most of the cooking, but as she got busier and busier in ministry and in her calling to preach to the nations, she had to rely on some pretty inexperienced cooks to "run the show." We were feeding people three times a day in those days, so running that kitchen was not for the faint of heart. It was and is a full-time operation. In those days, she wisely divided up the chores, and over time and some major Holy Ghost sifting, somehow I ended up being the resident cook. Getting to that resident stage was quite an experience.

As I shared earlier, to make Brother Miller's meals, Sister Miller literally had to teach me how to boil water. So obviously, Sister Miller had her work cut out for her. Please don't misunderstand. My mother tried to teach me; but she worked full–time, and I was a mess in the kitchen. Having my "help" was just more work for her. Thankfully, after years, I learned to make my mom's main specialty dishes—chicken corn soup, the best coleslaw ever, and Nanny's barbecue!

Sister Miller started teaching me, first how to peel vegetables, how to cut them, how to make casseroles, how to make Italian soup; and I stood at her side while she was making spaghetti sauce. She taught me how to cook noodles the Italian way, not the German way—boiled to death. I was definitely not used to being trained, and Sister Miller had a stern manner. I remember many times being in tears while she encouraged me to do things using her method. I want to stop right here and say that I was a bit of a spoiled brat, and a little tough love was totally in order. I needed to develop some backbone and not fall to pieces over every little thing that happened. It was good preparation for pastoring.

During the days, weeks, and months (years?) of Sister Miller's training, a lot of delicious food was served from our church kitchen. Unfortunately, though, during my "chef-in-training" times, there was also a lot of nasty food served that many people had to endure. Added to that was the challenge of cooking for men, or should I say "boys," who had just left Mommy's apron strings. I understand now, that frankly, no one cooks like Mom. So, with humor, I quote God's Word: "The trial of our faith is much more precious than gold," (See First Peter 1:7).

I think I neglected to mention that when I took over the cooking at the church, we were feeding about 15 to 20 people each meal. Plus, I was working day shift, 7 to 3, every day in Mechanicsburg, an hour away. The young lady who had been responsible for the cooking, decided to take a permanent vacation from our church, but even before she left, she was not in the state of mind to run the kitchen. To spare Sister Miller the torture of having her in charge, I volunteered for the cooking duties. My thought was, *Sister Miller was doing so much to help so many people, she needed to have her hands lifted.* Plus, I had not forgotten that God had told me to "*Help her.*" So, I would prepare the dinner meal late at night after most of the other chores were done or after a Bible study. Then I would place it in pans, prepped to cook or throw into the oven or microwave as soon as I got home from work the next day. While it was heating or cooking, I would set the table, set up the buffet line, and make sure Sister Miller had everything she needed. Promptly at 5:30 p.m., dinner was served.

So, I learned to cook, but not just cook. I, along with the whole gang of young people at that time, attended Sister Miller's home-grown but excellent etiquette class. Because Sister Miller had been professionally trained in etiquette, which included tasks like setting a table and decorating, we had the fabulous advantage of being trained by her. To be honest, I loved every moment of each lesson and found it to be "right up my alley." After she taught us etiquette (and boy did we need it!), she would arrange a lovely dinner where we would dress up in formal attire and go out for a five-course meal! When she taught the class again, we cooked the dinner, served it, invited a guest of honor (Lyle, Sister Miller's son), and I initiated him by dropping a baked potato right on his lap!

The element of serving, and doing so in an excellent manner, setting up a counter/buffet in a professional style, and cooking continued to develop, and was perfected during the course of time that I was in charge of the kitchen. I wanted to stay tied to that kitchen forever—it became my comfort zone. But as we all know, God orchestrates things to get us *out* of our comfort zone, and He was ready to "rattle my cage" with what came next.

Years earlier, Randy and Linda Ruth had reached out to a clan of kids at a local housing development, who then came to our church for a couple years. Then, slowly, they began to stop coming—all but one young man—Scott "Bubba" Brown. Scott was experiencing some situations in his life and consequently lived for a while with Pastors Ed and Nancy Schale. Then in time, he moved into the Hub while he finished school.

In the meantime, Bishop Miller's tug on me became stronger, and she started to request more and more that I travel with her. Many times, I was able to peel myself away; but again, this meant leaving my comfort zone, and I kicked and screamed against the revelation that it was time for me to step into something new. I had loved having no spiritual responsibility and rather enjoyed being a worker. But God had other plans, and Sister Miller knew it. She was relentless and would not give up.

At this same time, Scott graduated from high school, and shortly afterwards, Bishop Miller approached me with the idea of having Bubba be our chef. At first mention of it, I have to admit, I squirmed. Even so, Bubba hesitantly accepted the challenge, and Sister Miller said, "Don't worry, NAAAncy will teach you to cook." (I typed "NAAAncy" as I did, because that is the way Sister Miller always pronounced my name, with a long A-sound, and I have to laugh every time I think of it.)

I didn't really have time to teach Bubba to cook. Well, maybe we worked together for three days. Because as soon as Sister Miller knew I had a replacement, she grabbed me, and we ran. And why not? It was the perfect fit. She had already taught me to drive for her, how to care for the car, how to pack her suitcase, how to dress, and how to help her in ministry. And while I would drive, she would get ready for the meetings and enjoy some much-needed rest. Meanwhile, Bubba took over. And did he learn to cook. He had a lot of help from moms and others in the church, and eventually, he became a gourmet chef.

My favorite Bubba story was during the Shippensburg Fair one year. Every year, we would enter our best baked goods, jellies, and other food items to be judged at the Home Products portion of the Fair. We all knew that Bubba's Italian cream cake was absolutely delicious, and so we begged him to make one and enter it in the contest. He agreed and baked the cake, but then, threw it into the refrigerator uncovered and forgot about it. And there all weekend it sat in the fridge.

On Tuesday, I said, "Did you make the cake?" And he replied that he made it but hadn't added the finishing touches. Those of us in the room immediately jumped on his case and told him to "get over to the kitchen and finish that cake." So he did and submitted the cake with just minutes to spare before the deadline.

Lo and behold, the next day when the Youth Grand Champion Baker was announced, a sweet, young girl from our town took the honors. We were somewhat disappointed. But next, the Adult Grand

Champion was announced. And among all those farm wives and fabulous Mennonite cooks in the area, the winner turned out to be Scott "Bubba" Brown! With his picture on the front of the newspaper and a sweet smile on his face, he took home the biggest prize of all and for a cake that sat uncovered in the fridge for four days! Go figure.

Bubba was now our cook, and I firmly believe that during this time in his life, he developed an amazing ability to delegate. Many of the young ladies served as his sous chefs and his cleanup crew. "Bubba and the Flowers"—that's what we called them. Bubba not only cooked but he obediently continued Sister Miller's love of hospitality. So, with another chef in my place, the everyday kitchen at the church stayed in operation and we continued to feed families, singles, senior citizens, and the needy in our community.

During the coming years, we would rebuild and remodel our kitchen, add all kinds of professional equipment, expand, build walk-in freezers, refrigerators and eventually, under Sister Miller's guidance and encouragement, the kitchen ministry in our church would evolve into a successful, full-time, working, professional, yet extremely home-oriented kitchen. Because of Sister Miller's vision, our kitchen was not just open for a special dinner here and a special dinner there—it was *open*!

In time, Bubba would go to college, graduate, and move into other responsibilities, but God always provided people to fill in so that our kitchen standard remained at a tremendous level of excellence. Sue Brennan, Janice Hayhurst, Nancy Schale, Darlene Meyers, Karin Thompson, Amy Thompson, Scott Rhinehart, Karen Wiser, Johanne Thompson, Sam Wiser, and Sammy Wiser are others, who over the course of time, have been a part of the kitchen ministry—a true ministry.

Fulfilling Sister Miller's vision, our kitchen ministry includes a working everyday kitchen, a home-like atmosphere, special events, and parties that compete with a five-star resort. Plus, this ministry reaches out to the needy—something that Sister Miller had always done since I walked in the door. For more than 40 years now, we have been involved in the food pantry ministry. Every church Bishop Miller has been a part of, either in founding or establishing, has functioned in nearly the same way. She had an amazing ability to make a church a home, and that is precisely why people love our church so much. It's also the reason why the rumors in our town have taken on a life of their own and still raise their evil heads from time to time.

Bishop Miller making spaghetti sauce

And there was canning...

Carrots from our garden

I probably picked these green beans

Training the next generation

Bubba Scott Brown,
Grand Champion Baker at the
Shippensburg Fair

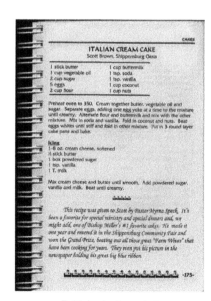

Bubba's winning recipe!

Our professional kitchen

Chapter Eight

"TELL ME LIES, TELL ME SWEET LITTLE LIES"—FLEETWOOD MAC

No weapon that is formed against thee shall prosper; and every tongue that shall rise against thee in judgment thou shalt condemn.
(Isaiah 54:17a KJV)

I had not been coming to our church for very long when Sister Miller shared an amazing story with us. When I first heard it, I was not completely sure that I believed it, but I kept that opinion to myself. No matter what I felt at that time, it was the *true* story of Sister Miller's capture in Ghana, Africa by the Fetish and the miraculous way she escaped a stoning in Prampram, where we now have our Training Centre. We all realized that you didn't have to be around Sister Miller long to know that she was animated, preached like a house on fire, *and* her life's stories and travels could easily be put into a movie. They were that entertaining! We would sit for hours listening to her teach, and often laced within her words were the tales of her adventures on the mission field. It was fascinating!

It was also the kind of stuff that could definitely make people—anyone who didn't like her, our church, or the Gospel—talk. And they didn't say kind words. Combine those stories, which were many, with the goings on in our church during the influx of the Jesus movement and hippie days, and you've got plenty of material to twist and spread rumors. I'm trying to imagine that talk of this nature happens in other churches to an extent, because, let's face it, churches that preach the Gospel represent truth, and truth has an enemy—the devil. Unfortunately, his greatest tool can be disgruntled people and their mouths.

Sister and Brother Miller had already endured a huge barrage of lies that had been spread about the church in the late 50s and 60s. While they were in Cuba, Sister Miller had placed another leader in charge. He must not have been a very good gatekeeper, because heresy, false teaching, and sin invaded the pristine spiritual walls of Deliverance Temple under his watch. At times like these, a lot of innocent people are injured, and sometimes, irreparably deceived when they are led astray by leaders who have listened to the wrong voice. Unfortunately, once some of that damage is done, it's done.

Testing our resolve during the days of the late 80s was a new set of rumors, begun by another group of disgruntled former members. Sister Miller was a tough cookie, and even after her husband passed away, she never came off as a helpless widow. While I am sure she was hurt inside, and deeply missed Harrison, the pain rarely showed on the outside. While taking care of her flock, she didn't have a lot of time to mourn. Even so, during those days we saw several powerful, intelligent, charismatic people come and go, within the church, who managed to start some extremely damaging rumors about Sister Miller and our church. Watching how she handled all this was a great lesson for all of us, even though we know she was deeply hurt by their unkind words.

One particular rumor that took wings and flew pretty far was one word: cult. That one always made me scratch my head, but I guess you can believe anything if you want to. Having lived around Sister Miller day in and day out, I can testify she was the *least* cult-like of any leader I have *ever* known. I know that sounds a little strange to any minister friends of mine, but hear me out.

Sister Miller lived among us *day in, day out.* We saw her reactions to tons of situations and countless people. I struggle to remember a time when she acted inappropriately or in a way that did not "become" the Gospel. Did she get angry? *Yes*, at the enemy and his works! Maybe I should clear that one up, too. We can point the finger at war and say, "That's the devil," at murder and say, "Look, that's the devil," at stealing and say, "That's the devil!" But when someone courageously looks at the people who have allowed the devil to work through them and says, "That's the devil!" all of a sudden, we have to be nice to the devil. See what I'm saying? Paul looked at the Pharisees and called them, "whited walls." Peter said to Ananias, "Why has satan filled your heart to lie?" Unfortunately, when people compromise their beliefs, ministers who hold them accountable and boldly stand for the truth then look radical. I believe, while sitting under Bishop Miller's ministry, we personally witnessed her confronting evil, and yes, sometimes that evil was in others, and sometimes, I found that it was in *me.*

I share all this to set the stage where I can unveil the truth that will fend off some of the ridiculous rumors that reared their ugly heads during this time in our lives. Maybe it's a little of "What the heck?" and a shaking of my own head. At the time, these tales truly set us apart from most of the churches in our town. Believe me, to us these rumors were far from a badge of honor, but I feel the need to address these distortions, given how deeply they affected our church and especially its local mission. Following, I address the most infamous hearsay and fabrications:

- "Sister Miller kidnapped our son."

  This is a rumor we didn't hear until years later after it was spread. When we did, we heard it through a minister friend of Bishop Miller who told her that "right out of the former member's mouth" spewed this lie. I'm not sure how I never saw this child running around the church, when I happened to live there during the time of his supposed "kidnapping," but I can assure you, Sister Miller had plenty on her plate. She didn't need the care of a child on top of everything else

- "There is a bridge inside of that church. When you walk over it, you have to stop sinning, but when you leave and walk outside, you can do anything you want to."

  I know where this one came from. Back in the day, we had a "bridge" in our sanctuary that reflected our Conference theme—"Building Bridges to Repair the Breeches." Add to that some very creative storytelling and—bam!—you've got a rumor that spread far and wide. I have to admit, Bishop Miller established themes for Conferences that sometimes required "revelation" to understand. Once you got it, it was exciting, but anyone who didn't understand where she was coming from could possibly be like, *Whaaat?*

- "When you go to *that* church, you have to hand over your paycheck."

  This is downright ridiculous. I cannot in my wildest dreams imagine how anyone would come up with this one *except* for the fact that over time, we have assisted, in a professional manner, a good number of young people who had no clue how to handle money or finances. Some of those kids lived here, but paid no rent and no money for food. *But* they were encouraged to, and did pay, their outstanding bills, their police fines, and other personal obligations. Their money was being managed by one of our trustworthy financial advisors within the church. On this point, Bishop Miller was way ahead of her time. Today, it is not uncommon for young executives to employ financial advisors who literally tell them where their every cent is to be spent. *Plus,* they *give* them an allowance to help them save money.

- "You can decorate your house only according to the way they say you can."

This rumor may have gotten its start from the generous way Sister Miller always helped others. Early on, I do remember a struggling young couple who moved into a "less than desirable" house. We received permission to "fix it up" for them. It was to be a surprise, and so we picked out a very simple design of wallpaper and paint colors. I'm not sure if that rumor was rooted in jealousy, or what, but nonetheless, this may have been its ugly beginning. By the way, the couple wept when they saw what we did to help them. They were thrilled!

- "Sister Miller was a defrocked nun who was expelled from the Catholic faith."

Sister Miller was raised in the Roman Catholic Church, but she was never defrocked—because she had never been frocked! She and Brother Miller were married Roman Catholic and later joined the Assembly of God Church because it suited them better after they accepted Jesus as Lord and Savior. She was never a nun, although she had ministered in several Abbeys over the years.

- "The church owns all the houses that its members live in."

In the Bible, the Levites lived around the Tabernacle where they served. Sister Miller loved this teaching because it sounded so much like the Oasis of Love Church. Over time, people who wanted to serve at and attend our church, seemed one by one to buy houses nearby. This was far from a forced action. The church was the center of their spiritual and social lives, and by living closer, they were saving themselves gas and time. The church does not own those houses. However, the church has purchased properties and has also sold properties. Today, the church owns one house where parishioners live, and it is used as an outreach opportunity.

- "They perform sacrifices in that church on the weekends."

Really? First of all, anyone who knows Sister Miller knows she could not hurt a flea; she loved animals and people! She was content to let God do the judging there, no need to sacrifice them. As for the rumor, our kids answered this one in high school by sarcastically saying, "Sacrificing on the weekends? No…it's just every other weekend." Ridiculous!

- "Their kids aren't allowed to date."

Well, this is one rumor that may have some merit. I ask with a smile on my face—the way kids "date" today, should they be allowed to date? We believe in holiness, and we believe there is absolutely no reason to date 40 people and slobber all over them before you find the right one. Each time you get hurt, you get more desperate. So, I guess when our pastors and parents ask kids to exercise some godly restraint, it can't be all bad, can it? We also have a bunch of folks who saved their first kiss for marriage. Ask them if it worked out for them. You'll love their answer. The way I look at it, a relationship based on physical affection early on cannot be good. We *do not* teach "you cannot kiss" as a doctrine. I recently told a young man who was inquiring about this same subject that this is merely a suggestion, not a doctrine. Whether they listen to the suggestion or not will neither persuade me to marry them or not marry them—either way.

- "Bishop Miller is a witch."

If the devil wanted to keep people from coming to our church, this was a good rumor to perpetrate in a small conservative town like Shippensburg. In the early 1970s, this one made the rounds on campus. It just so happened that the campus fellowship was having a Halloween Party at the Deliverance Temple hosted by Kathy Speck, now Pastor Kathy. Kathy had also invited a dear friend who had actually heard this rumor, so she was hesitant to even come. Yet she saw that Kathy was such a light for the Gospel! However, it didn't help Sister Miller's cause at her choice of an outfit that night—she came to the party dressed like a witch! (Yes, God, You do have a sense of humor!)

You may wonder why I felt it important to address some of the rumors we walked through with Bishop Miller. The truth is, through all of these rumors, Sister Miller handled it like a pro and never gave us the opportunity to be "haters"—because she was not one herself. The Bible is clear that "those who live godly in Christ Jesus shall suffer persecution." (See Second Timothy 3:12.) It's how we handle the persecution that counts. Living through these rumors and falsehoods that were out there about our church was good for us and for all of the kids who had to endure hearing it, even from teachers in the local schools. Jesus said, "For My sake, they will hate you." (See Matthew 24:9.) Sister Miller often said, "Let's just make sure that if they have to talk about us, that they have to tell lies." Those rumors fit that category well. They were simply the false inventions of some very creative, unhappy people.

Fetish

Chapter Nine

CALLED TO THE NATIONS

Pray ye therefore the Lord of the harvest, that He will send forth labourers into His harvest.
(Matthew 9:38 KJV)

For me, one of the most interesting, and I guess I can say, exciting parts of living with a missionary has involved the inner workings of where Bishop Miller travelled to, why she was going, how she was going, when she was going, and how she got ready to go. I can honestly say that the reason I was being trained to "minister" was to someday be Bishop Miller's successor. Being where I was, at the time I was (working and living in the church full-time) was an *invaluable* way to learn the ropes and the many layers of responsibilities that have to do with international and domestic travel.

It certainly had to be a challenge for Bishop Miller to teach me. I can picture, like in a comedy movie or cartoon, her standing against a wall, continuously banging her head on that wall, the entire time saying, "God, I prayed for laborers. But what did You send me?" At this point, I have to admit to a weakness, which I definitely battle at times. I love to learn new things, but only as long as it involves something that I like to do. There were many, many times that I did not like the instruction Bishop Miller was giving or the method she was using. But today, I am ever so thankful for both, because as I allowed her to instruct me, she pulled me out of my comfort zone. Little did I know of the number of "Nancys" I would also, one day, be privileged to instruct along the way. I learned from what I felt was a comfortable as well as an uncomfortable experience.

Talking about Bishop Miller's vast experiences traveling the world, I am thankful to have had the opportunity to travel with her, but it was also a grand experience "staying by the stuff" at home, helping her prepare for all those trips. Every experience with Bishop Miller could have been a college course, and I gleaned a lot by simply being observant.

It was Bishop Miller's practice to use the service of travel agents, and when I was with her, she always visited the one located at the old Camp Hill Shopping Center. I was fascinated when I made the journey with her and paid attention as she orchestrated her travels. As time went on, I was given the privilege of calling the agency for her.

At the beginning, I was afraid of my own shadow and needed Sister Miller to literally sit right beside me in order to teach me the "how, when, and what" as I made every phone call. It was unbelievable how afraid I was to make those calls, but because she had lots of patience and the faith that I could do it, over time I became her travel agent. Then I learned how to save points for her, not only with the airlines but with American Express as well. Additionally, in those days you could fly business and take a companion with you. The rewards were great, but still, a lot of times your points would expire. But even then, we learned how to work around that.

I was fascinated with the places where Bishop Miller traveled (which are listed in an addendum at the end of this book). Believe me, though, at first I had no desire to go anywhere, especially Africa. But interestingly, that perspective also changed with time. For now, I'll simply state that she traveled to the continents of Africa, Europe, South America, North America (including Canada), Asia, and Australia; and some of those continents, she crisscrossed pretty extensively. Antarctica was the only continent that she never traveled to. I can just picture Bishop Miller—that "little hot tamale," preaching, locked up in one of those "polar ice stations." There would have been enough Holy Ghost power to melt the ice cap! Actually, I can really envision her at the head of a sled-doggie team trotting across the ice; they would have been the most spoiled sled dogs on the planet!

Why did she travel to those faraway places? For one thing, Bishop Miller was an apostle, and apostles plant churches and aid the ministry. She also functioned as an evangelist and teacher—those ministries are needed worldwide. Many of those who had the opportunity to somehow hear Bishop Miller, or visit our church, or was blessed by the fruit that she was able to produce over the course of her many years of ministry, began to invite her from wherever they lived to minister in their church.

Another reason Bishop Miller ended up all over the world was that her gift made room for her. Bishop Miller's most honorable characteristics were her integrity and knowledge of the order of God. She knew how to conduct herself in someone else's house (church) and never stepped on another minister's toes, or usurped authority over them. She acknowledged that she was the guest, and he or she was the master of the house. She always told us, you don't walk into someone else's house, open the refrigerator and sit down, and eat without being invited. She would not prophesy, pray with, or speak in private with any church members or guests, or anything like that, without permission from the pastor. If she was given a time limit, she stuck to it; she could be trusted. She had friends in ministry from many countries (again, please see the list at the end of this book). They sent her letters of invitation and continued to ask her to come to them to minister. Doors were opened for her because of these great attributes.

A man's gift makes room for him, and brings him before great men. (Proverbs 18:16 NKJV).

Bishop Miller also functioned as a true missionary. She called herself a missionary, but not because she preached in a foreign land. Rather, she knew that in order to reach people of a different culture, you needed to reach them at their level, in their culture. She had no trouble eating the local food in a different nation or wearing the local dress. So that she would not offend, she watched others and learned how things were done in their culture before barreling ahead, doing things the "American" way. If she had to sit on the floor, she did it. That alone endeared her to many. Something she really drilled into us was noticing the unmistakable respect that many other nations held for the elderly. You can determine how "civilized" a nation truly is by observing how they treat those who are old. I'd say that in many cases, America is in trouble over this one.

Actually, we ministers would do well to conduct ourselves according to the standards listed above. When you preach in someone else's "house," make a concentrated effort to fit in to the way they do things; don't stand aloof like you are special. Get involved, be among them, be a part. These actions will help others to better receive the message God has given you. Just saying...

In the 80s and 90s, Bishop Miller traveled as a member of the Alberto Motessi Evangelistic Team. During her travels with this team throughout Central and South America and the Caribbean nations, many times she would teach seminars during the day. In the evening, her job was to warm up the crowd and prepare the way for Brother Motessi to preach the message and deliver the all-important altar call. Brother Motessi said he could not have done it without her by his side. During her days ministering with Alberto Motessi and his team, she stood before more than 100,000 people in some of those meetings. She always gave respect and honor to those she was representing and especially to the main minister who had invited her—Reverend Alberto Motessi, who is known as the Billy Graham of Latin America. The only time I know of that she disagreed with Rev. Motessi was when he lightheartedly felt she had done too much shopping and he vowed to cast out the "shopping spirit."

When she travelled, she was easy to take care of and didn't require much. She never asked for anything fancy and was always willing to share her space with someone else. She slept in huts in Africa, dorms in Australia, tents in South Africa; and only God knows what other kinds of places she stayed in to take the Gospel to the nations. She considered herself a servant, but in many cases, she was blessed to stay in the "best of the best" as a gift from those who had asked her to minister. She had paid her dues, and she did her best to teach us to do the same.

When we host guests within our own homes or at the church, we are taught that the guests should have the best place to stay. That's something very valuable that Bishop Miller shared from her experiences, and it's something that we try to pass on to our young people today. We teach our kids to move out of their rooms, if they can, in order to accommodate others, even as we older folks have moved out, sometimes sleeping on the floor, when hosting our guests.

Most of the time Bishop Miller traveled on coach class in planes, but in later years, we demanded that she travel business class. In her early years, she also traveled by car, bus, train, camper, semi-truck, and even motorcycle! In West Africa, she rode on a lorry with goats and various other creatures. She did mission work by fishing boat in Japan, rode gondolas to preach in Italy, in Africa she rode elephants for fun, and straddled a camel in Israel—just to say she did it. I almost forgot that she once rode a horse in Costa Rica to get to a mountain church meeting. In her 80s, she ascended to a very high altitude, way above sea level, in a dilapidated van, where she was not only the oldest, but the only one who did not suffer from the effects of that high altitude.

There was no real rhyme or reason to the seasons of when Bishop Miller would travel or where. There were times that she tried to gauge trips to Africa or South America according to times of more favorable climates, but that never made her all-out change her mind if she knew she was to go. I do remember reminding her that she might encounter several climates on a trip, like flying from the U.S. to Brazil, to South Africa, to Portugal, and back. But she was always a light packer, took detergent to keep her things clean, and was a real expert at coordinating her clothes for multiple uses.

When Bishop Miller was anticipating a trip, about a month before her travel dates, I would begin to see long lists lying around her apartment. Most of the time she stockpiled supplies, and she was always sure to take along some special "hostess" gifts for anyone with whom she might stay. She was ever cognizant of the weight of things, and in the course of time and with lots of patient instruction, she was able to train me how to shop for her. When Bishop Miller travelled abroad, many times she appeared on television. Consequently, she did try to take along some dressier-type clothes. She always looked like a lady and wore tastefully modest and lovely outfits.

At one period of time, I worked at a very nice women's clothing store in Chambersburg. As the owner began to trust me and understand Bishop Miller and the caliber of person she was, she allowed me to choose clothes for Bishop Miller and take them home for her to try on. Then I would take a check the next day for the ones she had chosen and return the others. It was a cool job. I loved working there, and I enjoyed picking out Bishop Miller's clothes. They weren't clothes I would have chosen for myself, but I knew what would appeal to her. I often told her, because she worked for the King, she had a right, like the queen of England, to have a personal shopper. And I was the appointed one.

Then there was the packing. Bishop Miller trained several of us to assist her as she packed her clothes for her trips. In later years, I watched the video, "One Year at Windsor Castle," filmed about one year of the comings and goings of the English Royals; and I was astounded to discover that the way we were instructed to pack Bishop Miller's luggage was *exactly* the way the Queen's luggage had been packed. They used gobs of tissue paper to prevent creases from appearing in the freshly pressed clothing. Believe it or not, many of those clothes returned home just as well-preserved.

Bishop Miller would pile her clothing, piece by piece on her bed. Then, I would recruit Angelique Brown to assist me at delicately folding every piece with tissue paper and placing all items in the suitcases. Every liquid had to be double-checked, tightened at the cap, and then taped to assure it made it across the ocean without leaking. Bishop Miller very wisely also took snacks with her, such as cheese crackers and granola bars; and many times she took hard candy for children or as a boost of quick energy for herself. It was always my responsibility to be sure she had all these things, and I really enjoyed being a small part of this operation. I loved serving her.

I can't go on without talking about a very special part of Bishop Miller's missionary trips and acknowledging one very special person intertwined in this story. First, let me say that Bishop Miller traveled on many occasions all by herself. Because she was relatively fearless when it came to international travel, Sister Miller never seemed bothered by flying "hither and yon" alone. Now, to say she was altogether fearless, would be a wild misconception about her, but when it had to do with going into the highways and byways of the world to bring people to Jesus, nothing was going to stand in her way! But as Bishop Miller began to age, I noticed a certain hesitation in her to travel alone, and at that time, she began to look for those who could travel with her. In the 70's she took a group to Puerto Rico with her, and later on, she hosted several people to the Dominican Republic.

I remember here and there she would even try to take a relative along as a companion/helper, but even that didn't always work. To travel with Sister Miller, no matter how well you got along with her on the day-to-day, did not mean you were going to hit it off in the mission field. She was sent as God's servant, and unless you were prepared to serve, take a back seat to your feelings, and put aside what you wanted to do on the trip, you probably would not be as helpful as she needed you to be. This was to be no casual "vacay"; this was a trip ordained by God and full of purpose and sacrifice. Not everyone is as ready for that as they think they are.

I travelled a good bit with Sister Miller domestically and was thrilled when she took me on a few trips internationally early on, but when she began to trust in me to "stay by the stuff" at home with the church, it was almost impossible for me to travel with her. First of all, I had to take care of her dog. That was like being in charge of her son or daughter, but more importantly, I was actually beginning to "pastor" the church.

Meanwhile, it was a continuous drain for Bishop Miller to train and instruct people who she really needed to *help* her when she traveled, and she began to do some serious seeking. Eventually, she seemed to find the one who was permitted by his Pastor/Mom and Dad to accompany Bishop Miller—and that was her grandson, Art Speck. He was a perfect fit. He was willing, he was family, and he was "kind of" available at the time. While it was hard for Pastor Myrna and Brother Bursie to give up Art as their "right hand" at the church in Huntingdon so that he could travel with Bishop Miller, it also brought great relief to everyone to know that Art was with his grandmother as she traveled all over the globe.

It would be entirely unfair for me to presume that I could faithfully detail what it must have been like for a young man in his prime to give up what he did in order to travel with his elderly missionary grandmother. I can assure you, though, that these times were destined by the Lord Jesus to bring a refining and a greater purpose and direction into Art's life. I believe it was as the Bible states in Isaiah 41:15, *"Behold, I will make thee a new sharp threshing instrument having teeth: thou shalt thresh the mountains… and make the hills as chaff"* (KJV). Each of us needs to make ourselves available to God for His threshing so that we can be that refined tool in His hand, which He can use to bring in the harvest. During the years that Pastor Art (as he is now called) traveled with Bishop Miller, he gained an ability to fit in just about anywhere, and believe me, I know that takes some effort, humility, and sacrifice.

Many times, he and his grandmother shared hotel rooms to save money. Art was her "servant," who went for the food and ran other errands; and it was his job in all kinds of environments to keep records, videotape, take pictures, wash clothes, arrange transportation, and nurse Bishop Miller when she was not well. One time, he even had to help get her onto a toilet seat that was too high for her short legs. Now, that's a servant, and it's few and far between kids who would do what Art did in those days.

Basically, he did what I was doing here in Shippensburg, only he did it without assistance, in a foreign land, and out of his comfort zone. Pastor Art may someday have to write his own book, to tell his part of his grandmother's story. Until he does, keep in mind that those who serve, sacrifice, give of their time, and honor and respect those they serve will be blessed. Because of Art's faithfulness, honoring God, his mom and dad, and grandmother, his life is a blessed life.

He who receives a prophet in the name of a prophet shall receive a prophet's reward (Matthew 10:41a NKJV).

One of the HUNDREDS of planes that Bishop Miller rode to carry the gospel

Sister Miller in Japan

Sister Miller walking to the airplane with her family

What a pair! Bishop Miller and Art traveled the world together

Chapter Ten

THERE'S NO PLACE LIKE HOME—CLICK...CLICK...CLICK

Whereas you have been forsaken and hated, so that no one went through you, I will make you
an eternal excellence, a joy of many generations.
(Isaiah 60:15 NKJV)

Try to put this in perspective: Bishop Elvina E. Miller, a very seasoned minister, missionary, leader, teacher, prophet, evangelist, all-around "firecracker" for Jesus, is getting ready to leave for a three-month trip around the globe. As she walks out the door, she glances in my direction in a room full of 20, 30, early 40-year-olds, and she says one thing: "Keep the peace."

First of all, why was she looking at me?

Second, was something wrong with her? She was leaving the care of that which she raised since infancy, and has been entrusted with from Jesus, with *us*? She's leaving *us* in charge of the church?!

But that little lady had an assurance from God that those whose lives she had been speaking into were getting hold of something, and that, possibly, her going away and trusting us was the best thing to do in order to bring further growth in our lives. She believed we had enough "backbone" to get through difficulties and the faithfulness to survive at least a few months until she returned from her trip. So that last "attitude adjustment"—"Keep the peace"—shot through me like a sword—a two-edged sword. I knew if I didn't "keep the peace," I was to going get another "peace"—a piece of her mind—when she returned! I laughingly say now—that's how I learned the fear of God.

Bishop Miller's method while growing our church, as well as the group in leadership today, the nucleus of pastors and elders, was not necessarily a planned situation. But I can assure you, it was a God-thing. I think that as people and patterns fell into place, she just rolled with it and tried to be obedient. After all, she was a student of the Word and a certain portion of God's Word just seemed to fit what was going on in our church at the time. In a similar measure, it continues.

The first oddity about Sister Miller as a minister, which occurred to me early on, was that she lived in the church. The Oasis of Love Church had been set up in a way that while it might have been a little weird and not like any church I had ever attended, the pastors living there seemed normal. What I was used to was a pastor who lives away from or possibly next door to the church in a parsonage. You don't always see them on a bad-hair day, or in Bishop Miller's case, when you are running around the kitchen with curlers in your hair. But when I moved into the church, I quickly realized that Bishop Miller did not turn her Christianity on and off. She couldn't. Did I ever see her when she was upset, angry, or sad? Yes, as I shared earlier, she's human, but her Christianity was likewise on display during every kind of circumstance, day and night, and that's why she was able to convince so many others to become believers.

So along with raising up a normal congregation—kids growing up, getting married, having their own children, and so on, there were always certain ones of us, at any given time, who were single and living in the church. Sister Miller opened the door to many, and these were pivotal growth days that aided in establishing some of the main, vibrant, and life-giving outreaches that are the foundation of who we are as a church, even today.

If you equate the church to a home, it can really work. In a home, you have moms and dads; you have boundaries (at least you used to). Mom often has duties she fulfills where the children are concerned, and so does dad. In our church, it began to take on that kind of a life. It was totally unplanned, but it worked. God used various ones to take on the dad role, after Brother Miller passed away. And in time, because Bishop Miller travelled so much, various people filled in for the mom role, and eventually, the role seemed to fall on me.

Believe me, we have so many stories to tell, that as I am journeying through this writing adventure, I have to keep reminding myself to limit it to what people will actually understand and not take away something they are not intended to.

Because we had adequate accommodations, and always seemed to be adding more space to the church and the facilities, people were continuously moving in and out of the church. Where did they come from? They came from various places. Some just showed up. Yes, that is totally true. Some got saved, were needy, and moved in. Some came from prison—referred to us by prison chaplains. Some were brought in by their parents or their pastors. It was and is a motley crew. But God can make and remake us so that we aren't "motley" anymore. Bishop Miller always felt like the motleys were easier to work with, anyway—they knew they needed help.

One way this arrangement was particularly beneficial to Sister Miller was that with people living in the church facility, she didn't worry about someone breaking into her apartment and stealing her belongings. Plus, she always had a dog or should I now say, *we* always have a dog or two…or three! (As of this writing, it remains at two.) She didn't have to kennel any of her pets because there were those of us who loved them and willingly watched out for them. And Sister Miller was very pet-friendly!

But getting back to the subject—it was a great benefit for the church to have people living on the property. While other churches all around were experiencing break-ins and thefts, we never did. Our buildings were brightly lit until very late some nights, and after a rash of church arson fires in our area, we even established a night watch, which went until 6:00 a.m. every morning. Only recently have we scaled that back. Thinking back, we did have one break-in. It was the night Bubba and another kid were sleeping in the Educational Building in order to guard it during a construction project. Because they were asleep right in front of the door, the burglar had to, after he jimmied the door, step right over them before he attempted to steal Ed's guitar and a set of drums.

The other benefit of people living at the church was the opportunity it gave Bishop Miller to incorporate a training element to the people of our church, which was a great "fill-in" for many of us who either ignored or rebelled against what our parents had tried to teach us. This situation was a perfect teaching and nurturing ground.

Moreover, this was an area where Bishop Miller shined. She was a Mom of moms, and she loved to pass on all of the spiritual and natural skills that she had. She taught us everything from the ground up. I know today, many of the moms and dads within our church credit her for helping them become the loving and responsible parents they are today. I sit back and wonder, *How did she do it?* Somehow, she managed to corral, train, establish, and rehab some amazingly unsavory characters, and I was one of them!

Bishop Miller herself didn't have a ton of formal training. She did not graduate from high school; however, that was not uncommon during the days when she was growing up. When she learned to read, she became even hungrier for knowledge, and then became an even more avid reader. She inhaled learning and was a lifelong student. She didn't always pronounce things properly, but it didn't bother me. I was looking at the vessel, and no matter how it was said, what was coming out of that vessel was good stuff!

Bishop Miller continuously acknowledged her shortcomings and was happy to have a group of people in the church who were more educated than she was. She was pleased to be able to have those who could fill in where she lacked, and it only added to the amazing common sense and natural knowledge that she had acquired about so many practical things. Keep in mind, she and Brother Miller had successfully run a household, raised two very qualified and wonderful children, and was a great motivator, without all the book learning.

With all that common sense, Sister Miller set things into an order in our church. She had a real desire to establish a school of some kind, a training school, a Bible school... whatever. But in the meantime, she did a great job as she established some rules for those of us who lived in the church. She made copies of those rules, asked some of us to duplicate them, and hung them in each room where someone was living. I'm not sure if I still have a copy filed away somewhere, but to generally describe those rules, I don't know one kid today who would abide by them, not even the children in our church. I guess it was for a special time.

Lately, I have had to write out some new "coordinates" for some kids who have moved into the church, and I found myself thinking through the new rules saying, "Times are different, Nancy. Just remember, times have changed." I wish we could turn back the clock sometimes, don't you?

While living in the church when I was younger, we had an order for each day. First, we divided the breakfast chores. Someone would set the table, cook, and help with clean-up. Breakfast was always served at 7:00 a.m., and it included prayer and a time of sharing. Most of the time, Bishop Miller was there, establishing a precedent of how it was to be done, acting as Mom, and teaching basic etiquette like how to eat with manners, how to carry on conversations at the table, and how to dress. We sometimes had less than an hour to eat together in the morning, but that hour could sometimes be the longest hour of your life! But it was good.

When she wasn't there, either by choice or because she was away on a trip, I would have feared to change anything! I didn't want the ceiling falling down on me. Keep in mind, if we didn't learn something at breakfast, we had two other meals we had to look forward to in which to glean from Bishop Miller's vast knowledge and wisdom. No matter how you look at this kind of structure, you have to admit, this is how things used to be in every home. People ate together and shared together, and Mom and Dad were held in high esteem and trained the children. What Bishop Miller had established, without calling it that, was a Bible school, and it was up and running like a clock.

Next on our agenda for the day, once we cleaned up from breakfast and for those who did not have a job to go to, was building maintenance or daily chores. In my case, it was preparing the meals for the rest of the day, that is, unless Bishop Miller needed me for another task. Most of the time, we tried to plan the night before, for the following day, so I somewhat knew if I had much time to plan a full lunch or dinner, or if that meal had to be a quickie. If it was pre-Conference time, we were responsible for long lists of "things to do" in order to prepare the grounds and building. If it was summer, our responsibilities included grooming our grounds, planting thousands of flowers, or harvesting, cleaning, canning and freezing vegetables picked from the garden or gleaned from the Food Bank.

Summer also meant a lot of other work and activities that included serving at Creation Festival, the Shippensburg Fair Outreach, Vacation Bible School, and Day School. (Summers here are still always a whirlwind!) Fall meant prepping for our cold Pennsylvania winter and raking leaves, which I always felt was busy work that made no sense, because the leaves were all back the next day anyway. But I might add that it was good for us! Winter meant shoveling snow, and lots and lots of Bible studies! Bishop Miller made sure we didn't experience much down-time—she was amazing at "inventing projects." That is one ability I totally inherited from her!

But in each season, many things remained the same—the important things. A foundation was established in our lives. Those who had ears to hear and allowed themselves to be groomed were groomed. A superb and excellent work ethic developed in many young people, and a love for God and a love for His Church and for *our* church became our heartbeat. I have always believed, and have heard it taught, that you should believe you go to the best church on the planet. It's best, not because it's the biggest, fanciest, has the most capital, or the best sound system. It's the best because it's where God has called you and where you have allowed God to plant your feet.

When I speak of excellence, I could literally write chapters on how deeply that quality has been embedded in my being. I have not always done my best to be a person of excellence, but I thank God and Bishop Miller daily for elevating my game and for elevating the games of thousands here on this huge playing field that we call life! She knew that to have people following her, she could say, like Jesus did, "These are my disciples." We are to go out and make disciples, and they should reflect their master, leader, or pastor. Because of that attitude and because she elevated her game, she lost some people over the years. Hopefully, they found a church where they fit more comfortably. But Bishop Miller wasn't interested in making us feel comfortable; she was interested in making *us*. There is a *huge* difference.

We didn't sit down at dinner with messy hair or messy clothes. If we had body odor, she found a way to help us to correct it; if we had bad breath, she would quietly let us know. She taught us how to eat with grace, and not like we were eating from a trough! Then she watched us to be sure we were learning. If we talked too loud or too soft, laughed inappropriately, whispered, talked too much, didn't talk enough, she instructed us. You have to remember, this was, and is a "school." Bishop Miller herself had taken an amazing course on conversation, and if she had done it just for me, it was a significant improvement for me. I needed it!

If we received the instruction willingly, we could change. If we resisted it like a hard nut, the hammer may have had to come down again harder. It was always obvious if you could take it or not, because it showed in your response. Grownups are the same—we just get better at trying to cover up our rebellion, or we may act like we are agreeing, but deep down inside we are bent out of shape. Over time, people who got weary of changing found reasons to hit the road. All in all, the core of believers and families who have remained in our church is a resilient tale of successful people, successful lives, and established believers making an impact on our church, our town, and our world.

Throughout the years, our church established somewhat of a reputation as a "halfway house" type environment. During about a 20-year period, we received a continuous influx of people who were brought to our church for help with their lives, as I have already shared. There was one definite lesson that we learned through that time—if people don't want help, you're wasting your time. Some young people were forced to come by parents, pastors, or chaplains, and often, they seemed to do well in our strict, training, Bible-school type environment—for a while. But if deep down inside themselves, they saw no true need to change and were obeying the rules only because they had to, you might as well forget it.

So, in time and because of some new state regulations, which were actually a relief to us, we stopped taking in people under some circumstances. We still have several accommodations where we can house people on our property, but those arrangements are for long-term stays. The stories I could tell about that 20-year time period, however, could fill another complete book and probably provide enough material for a comedy series on TV. One particular person, who I will not name, called me "the guard" and Sister Miller "the warden." I guess to him, our environment was like a prison, but only in his mind. I found it to be totally freeing!

Let me share a few testimonies in brief that will clarify my points.

Several years ago, there were two kids, not my children, but my kids nevertheless who were always under my feet. Their names were Angelique and Melissa. Their parents began attending our church and were spending a lot of time with Bishop Miller. Well, the kids needed a babysitter—who ended up being me. Those kids grew up at my side. When they moved to Shippensburg and on to Walnut Street, it was worse! Their mom had more kids, and because Conference was coming, Bishop Miller wisely suggested that they be my two helpers after school just about every day. We literally started to do everything together. They came by after school, helped roll silverware, do dishes, and do whatever else it took to help me get things ready.

Obviously, they grew up, went through teenage rebellion, but stuck it out through thick and thin. Melissa found the love of her life—Kevin, they married, had children, and suffered great heartache (including the passing of their infant daughter, Sara, who was stillborn at full term). Melissa endured painful trials, but she continued to allow God to speak into her life. She never gave up and faithfully served at our church, loving on the ministry. She wasn't afraid to be called on at any time and continues to be a pattern of excellence that was set forth by Bishop Miller. Melissa never lived in the church (except for countless nights when she and her sister shared my single bunk bed with me). But she did give up a job for a period of time and worked full-time in our church instead. Those were the days. Ohh boy, those *were* the days! If you ever get a chance to meet her, ask her about the time she threw away my favorite pair of shoes. Ask her how I prophesied at Youth Group in a roundabout way that she was going to marry Kevin. Ask her what it's like to have Bishop Miller tell you to "shape up or ship out," and then not run away after she says it to you. You can ask her, because she's still here. She didn't ship out; she shaped up!

Melissa often thought she was "dumb." Not true! She just had a different learning curve than other people; she is a hands-on type of student. Every place she has ever worked has wanted her to stay, but every job became a stepping stone. She is beautiful, and she radiates Jesus. Now, years have passed, and after raising two children, she and her husband are living blessed lives. Melissa manages a major college rental complex and is "the Mom" there, faithfully serving the church, leading the youth here, leading people to Jesus there—just by being Melissa. She genuinely graduated from this Holy Ghost school. She didn't just attend here and there, then expect a diploma, and have a hissy fit because she didn't get one. She actually went through this entire "school" established by Bishop Miller and took every training step God pushed her to take. She stuck it out. She didn't just survive; she thrived. She's a winner!

Then, there was Angelique; and today, she is my right hand. After high-school graduation, she moved into the church to help me (and herself). I couldn't believe God was going to "make me" live with this kid.

But Bishop Miller had her hand in it, and she also prophesied one day that we would work together. Time went on, and Angelique moved out of the church and took a job with a local municipality. Eventually, God made a way for us to travel the world together. She is my favorite sidekick, next to Bishop Miller. God certainly has had His hand on her.

But like most young ladies, she, too, had a dream of being married, and she found herself in love with her best friend, Bubba. She watched Melissa walk down the aisle and saw her two other sisters get married as well. Bubba and Angelique had been best friends for years and finally had the nerve to tell Bishop Miller they were in love. It surprised only a few, but Bishop Miller wasn't convinced. After the meeting which I happened to be present, I had to agree with her—they were not ready. They were very disappointed, but they threw no fits. They did not sit down and pout; they dug in and served.

Time went by—it seemed like years. I was beginning to see the writing on the wall and felt this thing had to happen. Meanwhile, Bishop Miller was beginning to experience what many do in their 90's: she was fading. I knew Angelique and Bubba wanted her approval to marry. I knew they *needed* her approval. So, I talked with Angelique's mother, Sara, and she approached Bishop Miller. Then I approached her. It was a back-and-forth month filled with emotion, and the response we were getting from Bishop Miller wasn't always the same. Eventually, Angelique and Bubba met with her another time, and she said "no" once again to the marriage. Then they met with her again. At that momentous meeting right before Easter Sunday, the word finally came which they were waiting to hear. "Yes." Without saying another word, we moved on it.

Angelique and Bubba were engaged the next day, on Easter Sunday, in front of friends and family. The anointing of God filled that house, and we cried. We screamed. We giggled. We rejoiced. They were engaged! Then in three months, they were married. Angelique was 39, and Bubba was 38. Because the clock was ticking, Logan was born when Angelique was 40. Then, after several miscarriages and a cancer diagnosis, at the age of 44, Angelique gave birth to Carson!

I was there for both births, cheering them on, giggling, laughing, praying. Today, they are living a blessed life—a new home, a new job for Bubba, and both are still serving, still being faithful. No one went "AWOL" when they didn't get their way. No complaints. They totally respected the ministry and were willing, even if they heard a "no," to live life single and live without one another. But that was only a test. God is never early, nor is He ever late. It wasn't the school of hard knocks; it was the school of the prophet of God. Who knows what we must go through when we must go through it? He knows our future; He's preparing us for it.

There is another young man I would like to share about. His name is Sam. Sam came from a lovely family that had deep roots in our church. His father, Sam Wiser, Sr., has been here for most of his life. His mom, Karen, was grafted in after her marriage to Sam Senior. Sam Sr. and Karen have four children, and all of them are serving the Lord. Sam Jr. was their only son, and he was a little introverted as a young boy. His parents raised Sam and his sisters in our church. They attended all the services and were involved in the life of the church in many ways.

Sam Jr. had great qualities, but when he was young, he was made fun of by some of the kids from our church. That's never pleasant, but Sam continued to stay plugged in and was always an obedient kid. Did he ever question anything at our church or resist his parents? I'm sure, if he was normal, he did. That's part of life. But he stayed accountable and stayed plugged in. He was part of every drama and music activity and was an integral part of our dance team. Sam had great potential—that was obvious; it just needed to be pulled out.

As Sam gained confidence, he began to find his voice. He excelled in high school and served as a class officer. Then he entered Shippensburg University and served in student government and as class president. After college, he was admitted to law school. Through all this time and throughout his education, Sam remained faithful to the church. (There is something about that quality that causes me to jump for joy and brings great peace to any pastor: trustworthy people.) Eventually, Sam graduated from law school and received an offer to join a local firm.

In addition, Sam is married with children, and while he is very busy with his work, he remains actively involved in the church and maintains the same level of faithfulness that he always has. He leads projects, assists with worship, and has been a tremendous blessing serving as our legal counsel here. Sam has many talents. He can cut hair, arrange flowers, do landscaping, cook, and is an avid hunter, when he has time. But the quality I admire the most is what I call "true blue." I completely trust him. He sat at Bishop Miller's feet, and now he sits at mine. He has honored his family, and he continues to honor God. Did everything go his way? No, it did not, but he didn't cry over it. He pressed on and is becoming what God has called him to be. In my mind, there is no limit to what Sam may one day do.

Bishop and the gang

Honey Bun gets a hug before the
etiquette class

Bishop speaking words of life to these children

Angelique, me, and Melissa

My young helper, Angelique

Little Melissa

Angelique and Melissa being silly

Sam and Becky at their wedding

Chapter Eleven

HOW DID SHE DO IT?

"We have young people who come to our church and say, 'Use me, Lord!' Then a few months later, they leave the church and say, 'I felt used!'"
– Pastor Carl Lentz, Hillsong, NYC

He will make the Levites clean. He will make them pure, like silver is made pure with fire! He will make them pure like gold and silver. Then they will bring gifts to the Lord, and they will do things the right way. Then the Lord will accept the gifts from Judah and Jerusalem. It will be as it was in the past—as the time long ago.
(Malachi 3:3-4 ERV)

Recently, I had an opportunity while in the country of Ghana to describe how the ministry team in our church works. I consider it unique, awesome, natural, and supernatural! With the layering of teaching and training, and the blessing of being able to put all of that to work, I am always extremely proud of and thrilled at how our worship team and staff have developed over the years. We have had several groups of ministers visit our church to discover the "formula" and learn about Bishop Miller's plans for building such a family-oriented, interactive, and caring church. She had no book but the Bible, and actually no "formula," except common sense and a love for God. That's how she did what she did. Plus, after all, don't we see a pretty clear picture of the church in the Book of Acts? I am hoping you have acquired a better knowledge of how the church developed by reading what I have shared so far. Even so, I think delving into it a little deeper may explain how Bishop Miller was so successful at *building* our church.

The Family That Prays Together, Stays Together

It is unusual for these times (but doesn't seem to be unusual in our church) that many of our families have stayed and prayed together. A family will form by marriage, then children come along. Those kids marry, more kids come along, and some stay connected in one church. The examples of those who have put their roots down and have stayed or returned to Mom and Dad's church include some amazing servants in our church. The layering of faithfulness and the foundation of that faithfulness goes back, I believe, to their first example—Sister Miller. Sister Miller's children served God, and in turn, their children served God. Continuing the legacy, her great-grandchildren have also chosen to serve God.

Some may claim that this simply points to the children being mindless goons, but I beg to differ. They have witnessed incredible strength, fortitude, and success in individual lives who have been worthy of following. I have several friends who grew up in families of ministers. Sadly, their kids, while being independent thinkers, also seem to have gone in a multitude of directions spiritually, to the chagrin of their parents. I look at them and am amazed at how such seemingly "solid" believers could produce such independent, rebellious, and untamed kids. Not all independent thinking is bad, but if it aligns with "independent-so-we-can-do-what-we-want-without-fear-of-condemnation" or more plainly "independent-so-we-can-sin," that's when I have a problem with it.

In our church, a few dedicated families, some who have been at our church forever and others who came in with the second wave of revival, are faithfully serving God, and their children in turn (married or single) have chosen to stay around and allow themselves to be planted in the house of the Lord. A fruit tree once planted and fertilized, produces fruit. See Psalm chapter 1.

This scenario can produce two offspring: either religious, self-righteous kids or sold-out kids who are hungry for more and want to see their offspring raised in the environment that nurtures dedication and faithfulness to God. I am thankful that we see much of the latter.

Jack of All Trades, Master of A Lot!

Bishop Miller was definitely skilled in many areas. Because of those skills and the skills of her husband, in the early days especially, they took the time to teach and train in abundance. When Bishop Miller asked me to write this book, I didn't really have much of an outline, but I did sit back and ask myself, "Can I do this?" Then, I thought of one story, and then another… and as you have already read, there are many.

During the time back in the early 1980s, macrame was a popular décor. Bishop Miller had this very unusual copper vase that she wanted to hang in her room, and she needed a macrame holder to be able to hang it. She gave me the vase and told me what she needed. I looked at it, and I knew it was going to take some maneuvering. I wasn't thrilled to even try, but I took the vase and began. After several hours and several failed attempts, I took it back to Bishop Miller and pronounced that I could not do it. She looked at me and said something I will never forget. "Nancy, I have never heard you say there was something you could not do." And that was all it took. I looked at her and replied, "Well, let me give it another try." Then I took it downstairs, and within minutes, it was done. I needed someone to believe in me, and when that happened, my attitude changed in a second. I *could* do it… if I wanted to.

Sister Miller must have prayed for laborers, but I think she could have been a little more specific. She should have prayed for "skilled" laborers. She definitely had a pile of eager workers who were itching to work for Jesus and for our church, but few knew how to do much in the way of the trades. She had cooks who couldn't cook, electricians who didn't know much about electric, gardeners who didn't know how to garden, painters who couldn't paint… the list goes on. But what she did have was a willingness from many of us, and she knew how to train us, as did Brother Miller.

For example, when something needed painted, she taught us how. She was a *great* painter. On one occasion before an event, we had some extra time to spare before we had to leave, and there was Sister Miller, wearing a long, white formal dress and outside painting a door. She was a great example; and if you were teachable, she would show you how it was to be done, then watch you to be sure you got it. I'm not even able to name all the things I learned to do under her tutelage. Keep in mind, she had others in the church who were eager to teach as well. Add that all together, and we became skilled at a lot of tasks.

We were blessed and able to use this fantastic training in our own families' homes, in other churches, in our town… you name it. We actually developed a reputation in our town as the church that was always involved in a project and one that was always lending a helping hand to someone or some organization. That's a good reputation to have. In time, we had to start saying "no" to some projects, because we were inundated with all of the things that we had committed to within our town. I titled this section, "Jack of All Trades, Master of A Lot!" which was the truth. And through the years, that training has served us well and likewise served up-and-coming generations, too. You can never know too much, but you can know too little.

This training stuff may not seem like it should be part of a ministry team or the building and putting together of a church, but you would be wrong if you assumed that. The interaction that took place as a result of training and instruction on every level shaped many lives, like the refining that the Scripture in Malachi chapter 3 speaks of (see the beginning of this chapter). Submission, doing a job someone else's way and not *your* way, and being stretched to learn, is vital in building ministry. If you have a worship leader that sings but won't get their hands dirty, you've got a shallow worship leader. How can you be sure they are teachable, trainable, and submissive? All of the teaching and instruction that went on at our church built character, which is the basis of ministry and is the foundation for the kind of leaders that Jesus expects. Think of the Scripture, "Occupy, till I come" (see Luke 19:13 KJV). That Greek word *occupy* means "to busy oneself with trade." *Get busy!* We are to busy ourselves until He comes.

A couple years ago, I was headed into a grocery store, walking through the parking lot, when I glanced ahead of me and noticed a car that belonged to a man who used to attend our church regularly. He and his family had left our church and over the years had had some pretty strong words with Sister Miller. I always got nervous when I saw him, because quite honestly, I never knew what was going to come out of his mouth or his wife's; they had both spoken out against Bishop Miller and our members in public places. Even so, I went into the store to pick up a few quick items. While inside, I caught a glimpse of this man, but he never saw me. I then paid for my groceries and left the store. The quickest route to my car was to go past his car, and for some reason, I glanced into the vehicle. What I saw is etched in my mind even today. The car was filthy and was filled with trash. I'm not talking about a cup and a couple of McDonald's wrappers from breakfast that morning. I'm talking about a dumpster worth of trash in the back and front seats! For some reason, I was not surprised. He hadn't stayed for the training. He was already an intelligent, well-spoken guy, and he had learned to preach, learned to spout off and prophesy, but he had never learned to clean his car. There's just something wrong with that. Bishop Miller jokingly would say, "Jesus even folded His grave clothes in the tomb; who do we think we are?"

We Are the World

Not very long ago, we drew a chart that illustrated the far-reaching "arms" that the members of our church have established in our community and surrounding areas. Like every good church, we feel we are to be beams of light, piercing through the darkness, bringing the light of the Lord Jesus Christ to many, many, many! After we looked over that chart, we were amazed that God had placed so many of our people in pivotal leadership roles, wherever they have found themselves, in their secular jobs or ministry callings. It was exciting! But why should we be surprised by that? From the very get-go of my relationship with Sister Miller and our church, I heard her drum beat—"You can only affect the world you are in!" As God said to Abraham, "Arise, walk in the land through its length and its width, for I give it to you" (see Genesis 13:17 NKJV). In other words, *spread out*. Take the Gospel wherever you are, and share it and its principles in whatever you do.

That simple lesson is a cry to each believer, to realize the power of God that exists within them to make an impression on the world. Everywhere we go, He goes with us. Elvina E. Miller, our leader and Bishop, believed that. She lived it at the hairdresser. She lived it in the shops. She lived it at the doctor's office. She lived it everywhere she found herself. Most importantly, she lived it away from the pulpit! She didn't turn her faith off and on. Likewise, we should represent Jesus at all times and in every place. For we are always being read by all men.

I repeat, we are the world, and our job is to *infiltrate*! Bishop Miller taught us as a church that whatever He has called us to do and allowed us to do should be done heartily as unto Him. She emphasized that we Christians should be the best businessmen, the neatest employee, the fastest waitress, the most honest lawyer, the most accurate accountant, the kindest nurse, the doctor with the most empathy, the friend you could trust. Need I say more? We live *in* this world; let's saturate it with the goodness of God.

I had the honor of driving in a vehicle with Bishop Miller for many hours and many miles. (And she helped me drive the speed limit, too!) In our travels, it was never unusual for her to help a hurting soul, pray for a hairdresser (yes, it was a gay man), witness to a store clerk, or melt at the sight of an abused animal. I witnessed her give money to the poor, and more than once she bailed me out when I was in financial straits. We are the world. Her goal, our goal, should always be: let's make it a better place. She preached it and did everything to make us see how important it was to live this way every day. I pledge to do the same.

Don't Be Afraid to Laugh

I am so very thankful that Bishop Miller had a sense of humor. Honestly, she was a fantastic teacher, preacher, and prophet, and along with all of her gifts of ministry, she could really crack us up! Some of her stories were unbelievable, yet they were true; and we loved her to tell them again and again. We would howl and laugh while we were being spoon-fed the Gospel through her fabulous stories of ministry. In addition, because she was not afraid to include humor in our services, quite honestly, we saw a few crazy ministry gifts spring out of us that were funnier than "Saturday Night Live." I really do not have the time or space to include them all, but over time, and with the advent of our "New Wine Cellar Coffeehouse," which was held once a month for almost 30 years, some of our skits and the characters in them became almost legendary. In fact, people drove for *hours* to come to our coffeehouse, which spawned at least five other coffeehouses that we know of. People really *laughed,* and while they were laughing, they were hearing the Gospel of the Lord Jesus Christ.

Bishop Miller was free enough to ride into church on a Harley, fly into VBS on a helicopter, dance with the kids in a costume, take up the offering from a golf cart, wear combat clothes in church, and she was not afraid to laugh with and at herself. That totally endeared her to me, for I have also always loved to laugh. Life should be full of it and so should church. At our church, if we get to know you well enough, during the service or in some other way, you will soon be included in the fun. And if we do include you, that's a compliment!

One of the funniest and most ridiculous episodes that has ever happened in our church, has to be shared here. Unfortunately, I cannot hide the name of one particular man because it is important to the story. We were hosting a special speaker, whom Bishop Miller had invited to our church. He was a friend of a friend and had been recommended to us, although Bishop Miller didn't really know him. His name was Buddy Makepeace. He was a wonderful man, and well, he was a little overweight… but again, a very, nice jovial man. As usual, I wanted to assist Bishop Miller, and before the meeting, as we talked, we both realized she was having trouble remembering his name… and she was the one who always introduced our guests. So we agreed that I would write his name on a piece of paper and make sure that it was written in plain, large letters, so that when it came time for her to introduce him, she would not goof up his name.

The service began, and Bishop was up front, sharing. Soon, the moment came when she was to introduce and name our guest minister for the day. I kept hoping that I would see her glance down at the paper I had placed there, knowing that what could possibly come out of her mouth may be a disaster. But she never glanced down. In her enthusiasm, she rolled right along and named not once, but twice, "the Reverend Chubby Peacemaker."

What was I to do? I tried with every bit of control I could muster not to laugh, but as I heard snickers everywhere, I was losing the battle. *CHUBBY PEACEMAKER!?* I did not laugh out loud, but was visibly shaking all over as I desperately tried to get a grip! When Bishop Miller called our brother to the podium, she *finally* got his name right, but it was too late. She sat down beside me, knowing I was losing it and said, "How did I do?" I looked at her and on the verge of hysterics said, "Not good." She began to laugh, then slapped me gently on the back as she encouraged me to try to get myself under control. Later in her apartment, she asked, "What did I call him?" I said, "Sister Miller, you don't want to know!" Eventually, though, I told her, and she was *mortified*. But again, we had a great laugh over that one, and many people still do. She was not afraid to laugh at herself.

Similarly, the "in-control" way that she handled so many things was amazing. One year, we were feverishly making salads to be displayed on the salad bar for our annual Conference. It was the day before the event, and we had been working all morning, cleaning and cutting up broccoli to make broccoli salad. When we were done, we had this massive, and I mean massive, bowl of broccoli salad ready to be taken across the street to our large kitchen and placed in the walk-in refrigerator. There were two young men there that day, assisting us, both of whose names were "Mike." The one man grabbed the huge bowl, and the other went ahead of him. Little did I know, they had just had "words." Let me be plain—they had an argument. The young man carrying the salad had had enough, and by the time they reached the end of the sidewalk, without warning, he thrust the entire bowl of broccoli salad right over the head of the other guy!

In a tizzy, I ran up the steps to report the unfortunate event to Sister Miller. I'm really not sure what I thought she would do… maybe yell at them? But instead, she looked up from her work and without flinching said, "Mike so-and-so probably needed broccoli salad thrown on his head." Boy, that was the truth, and we began to laugh. Back down to the kitchen I went… and more broccoli salad was soon on the way.

Don't be afraid to laugh.

Sister Miller and I planning something!

Bishop Miller, always in the middle of everything!

Chapter Twelve

THE LONG AND WINDING ROAD

*In You, Lord, I have taken refuge; let me never be put to shame. In Your righteousness, rescue me and deliver me; turn Your ear to me and save me. Be my rock of refuge, to which I can always go; give the command to save me, for You are my rock and my fortress. Deliver me, my God, from the hand of the wicked, from the grasp of those who are evil and cruel. For You have been my hope, Sovereign Lord, my confidence since my youth. From birth I have relied on You; You brought me forth from my mother's womb. I will ever praise You. I have become a sign to many; You are my strong refuge. My mouth is filled with Your praise, declaring Your splendor all day long. **Do not cast me away when I am old; do not forsake me when my strength is gone**. For my enemies speak against me; those who wait to kill me conspire together. They say, "God has forsaken him; pursue him and seize him, for no one will rescue him." Do not be far from me, my God; come quickly, God, to help me. May my accusers perish in shame; may those who want to harm me be covered with scorn and disgrace. As for me, I will always have hope; I will praise You more and more. My mouth will tell of Your righteous deeds, of Your saving acts all day long— though I know not how to relate them all. I will come and proclaim Your mighty acts, Sovereign Lord; I will proclaim Your righteous deeds, Yours alone. Since my youth, God, You have taught me, and to this day I declare Your marvelous deeds. **Even when I am old and gray, do not forsake me, my God, till I declare Your power to the next generation, Your mighty acts to all who are to come.** Your righteousness, God, reaches to the heavens, You who have done great things. Who is like You, God? Though You have made me see troubles, many and bitter, You will restore my life again; from the depths of the earth You will again bring me up. You will increase my honor and comfort me once more. I will praise You with the harp for*

Your faithfulness, my God; I will sing praise to You with the lyre, Holy One of Israel. My lips will shout for joy when I sing praise to You—I whom You have delivered. My tongue will tell of Your righteous acts all day long, for those who wanted to harm me have been put to shame and confusion (Psalm 71:1-24 NIV, emphasis added).

I could seriously conduct a Bible study for a year based upon Psalm 71, and it just happened to be one of Bishop Miller's all-time favorite Psalms. You can see why. I could slip her name in there in many of the verses, and it would fit like a glove. She would pick up her Bible and read that Psalm to us and it was for her. She had walked through so much. She had been lied about, accused. People tried to kill her, had mocked her. She had several near death experiences, but through it all, God was glorified and she rejoiced in Jesus, her Lord and Savior.

Her cry to God remained the same, but now on the cusp of old age, she could be heard speaking the words from verses 9 and 18 (NIV):

Do not cast me away when I am old; do not forsake me when my strength is gone.

Even when I am old and gray, do not forsake me, my God, till I declare Your power to the next generation, Your mighty acts to all who are to come.

The last 20 years have been amazing years. Although at times I felt like I was on the sidelines, watching a sporting event, experiencing all of the highs and lows as the score went in favor of my team, then the opponents, I would not trade these years for anything. The emotions, the anticipation, the hope!

Back in the 1990s, Bishop Miller traveled and returned to a place she had not been to for many years—Ghana, Africa. On one particular trip, she visited a town that had a unique and meaningful place in her history, the fishing town of Prampram. With her grandson, Art Speck, she journeyed to that area for the first time since she had held meetings there in the 1950s. During those meetings, she was captured by fetish believers, and they attempted to stone her. God delivered her through the hands of what we believe was an angel. She returned to the States with black-and-blue marks still visible on her arms, a leftover injury from the capture. (If you have not already done so, you must read Bishop Miller's book, *Captured in Africa*. It details the story of her capture as well as her journey back to Prampram.) It was an exciting time in her life; and after her deliverance from the fetish, she prayed for the king of that region. And many witnesses saw what happened and believed in Jesus.

It was the fulfillment of a dream to revisit that village and see what God had done as years had passed by, and it would answer the question—did anyone remember her and remember the capture?

On that amazing trip, she and those with her went from church to church throughout that fishing village on a Sunday morning. At one church, as she told her story, a believer stood and claimed that she had remembered the capture. Her mother had been one of the fetish priestesses who was there during Bishop Miller's encounter with the fetish. In fact, she was the one who had held Bishop Miller's arms while the fetish attempted to stone her. From what Bishop Miller remembered, Prampram was a place with very few churches and few believers. Upon her return, however, she found that the town was littered with churches, churches *full* of believers. How very exciting! How amazing! How miraculous!

Her excitement during that re-visit, at what she saw, caused a fresh desire in her to somehow do *something* that would benefit, as well as commemorate, all God had done since her time there in the 50s. Her mind began to work overtime, and by the time she returned to the States, all she could think of was going back to do something for that special town of Prampram. Should she build a memorial? What about a prayer chapel? Maybe an event center? Not a church, because there were plenty of churches in the town. But she was determined to do *something*!

In the meantime, Sister Miller returned to the States with yet another Prampram story, and we didn't quite know what to think. We were in the middle of drawing up plans to build an addition on to our building that would house offices and two apartments—one for Bishop Miller and one for me. Working on the plans for our building and trying to imagine how we could also do something abroad almost seemed impossible and was likely improbable. But I'll never forget the day she told the congregation what she was about to do. She was so determined! She didn't ask us for money to go forward; she told us she was going forward with it. She wasn't relying on anyone to help her get this accomplished; she would, if she had to, do it herself.

Soon, she traveled back to Ghana, and against my wishes, I accompanied her on the trip. God was gracious, and so was Bishop Miller. Her contacts from Prampram picked us up at the airport in Accra and took us very late at night to the fishing village. After a meet-and-greet with some local pastors, and a drink, we were taken to a hotel called the Sealane Hotel, where I did not sleep a wink the first night.

There was a scorpion in the room! Oh, I alerted Sister Miller to our intruder, but she rolled over and told me to go to sleep because we had a big day tomorrow. *Sleep?* I had to make sure I was alive to *see* tomorrow. So my first night in Africa, I laid awake all night listening to every new sound and waiting to be stung at any moment by that scorpion!

The next day, we met with several people and had dinner with those we were traveling with. Our trip was planned for three weeks; but I knew our tickets were changeable, and so I was interceding for a shorter adventure. What a brat I was. Bishop Miller met with the leaders of the town and petitioned them for land. When asked what the land was for, she prophesied the answer, "I want to build a training center." Consequently, the local officials granted her the land and agreed that they would let her know where that land would be located, and in the meantime stay in touch. We met with pastors again the next day, named the training centre The Oasis Interdenominational Training Centre (it was later renamed, International), drew up some "official" papers, and chose a motto: Living to Train, Training to Live. Most folks (including Pastor Art) didn't know that the motto was an adaptation of my "sorority motto" from college, but it really seemed to fit. When I coughed it up at our meeting with the local pastors, it was immediately agreed upon. Go figure.

The next day, we traveled on to another village, attended a meeting, and then made our way to another village, stayed for Sunday service, and then we were ready to come home! Bishop Miller was anxious to get home; needless to say, I concurred.

Our trip lasted eight days, and it was the beginning of something wonderful, the beginning of what would be a monumental shift in focus for all of our churches. This would be a lifetime achievement for Bishop Miller. The completion of the Centre would be the icing on the cake of a rewarding ministry and career for this amazing preacher.

After we arrived home, immediately Sister Miller wanted to put a stop to our construction project at the church, which we actually had not started. Quite frankly though, it was because of that project that we eventually went ahead with the Training Centre project in Ghana. Our men looked at Sister Miller and said, "Sister Miller, if we can't afford to build here, we certainly can't afford to do it in Ghana." They were right, and did we learn a lot about faith during that project! In the next six months, we began and finished The Annex on the back side of our church building, an addition worth around $250,000. We dedicated it, moved in before Conference, and were ready to tear into the project in Africa.

It was a very exciting time. We were back and forth with builders in Canada who had manufactured a building that would be perfect for Ghana, and one that was being used all over the world. We drew initial plans and drawings and were flying from north to south, south to north, negotiating and working on everything about the building in Ghana. Pastor Myrna and her husband, Bursie, were vital parts of this process as they accompanied Bishop Miller on many of her trips concerning the purchase and plans of the building. Meanwhile, Bishop Miller and Art went back to Ghana, to secure the land and begin to do work to prepare for the building. We also had to complete the work on the ground, which had to be done before the building arrived. This labor involved others from home who were skilled in moving dirt and other appropriate tasks for this job. No grass would grow under our feet!

I'll never forget the day when the men from Canada called to give us the price for the building. It would be $500,000. Bishop Miller never flinched; I wanted to faint. But her faith encouraged faith in the rest of us, and we began to raise money. Our churches are not mega-churches. We average around 100 people per church, give or take 25, so this project was *huge*!

In time, the land was firmly secured, and our men began traveling back and forth to Ghana, some going for what seemed to be years at a time. In the meantime, the land was prepared, and the piles of paperwork were complete enough to be established and recognized by the government in Ghana. This was a very *looonng* process. But, it had to happen before we could even attempt to begin to have the building and its contents shipped. It wouldn't take one shipping container; the building alone took seven shipping containers. While the workers were prepping containers in Canada, we began packing and sending containers to supply and furnish the Centre as much as we could from the port of Baltimore. Keep in mind, we were not shipping barrels. We were sending sea-containers, which would fit on the back of an 18-wheeler! It was a wild and crazy time.

We had made arrangements to pay an initial down payment on the building, but every once in a while, we were responsible to send in another payment of $60,000. Guess who was in charge of raising that cash? I was. We never missed a payment. But it wasn't only that expense; we also had to support and take care of all the folks who were traveling in groups back and forth to Ghana to help build. It was quite the time for raising funds, but we always had enough. It was miraculous!

Another matter we had to consider was housing. We could not and would not pay to stay in hotels for months or years at a time. It was imperative that we find somewhere to house our crew and Bishop Miller while she was in Ghana. It so happened that during one of Bishop Miller's trips, she was blessed to meet Ben Kusah and his wife, Salome. Ben was a successful architect who was from and still lived in Prampram with his family. Salome was very excited about the building of the Training Centre and was actually one of our first students. Salome and Ben lived in a large complex of very nice homes, one of which just happened to be empty. With three bedrooms and two bathrooms, this house would eventually become the answer to our housing needs until staff could move into the Centre.

One fact I forgot to emphasize—Bishop Miller was in her early 80s when she began this project. *Her 80's!* The mere fact that she was older was "hairy" enough to begin with, but the entire scenario had her family, our churches, and *me* in almost a constant state of panic and bewilderment. This woman was *driven* to get this thing accomplished! Nothing was going to stand in her way.

And so, Bishop Miller, surrounded by a cast of "thousands," descended on Ghana, moved in, almost lock, stock and barrel, while Pastor Ed, our leaders and I ran the church, raised money, and worked tirelessly to make it all come together. Bishop Miller would be gone for months, come home, go back, come home… the cycle continued. During that time, if you were able-bodied and willing, your time would come, and you would be recruited to become part of the work force who was making it happen in Ghana.

I was constantly searching for flight prices and raising money for flights… and became an expert at sending cash by FOREX as well as obtaining visas at the last minute. During that time, I also learned that I could drive to BWI, Dulles, Reagan, and Newark Airports with my eyes closed, and it was just about as easy for me to get to JFK! I had always loved to drive, so these trips were fun for me. In addition, I saw many, many people give up weeks and weeks of vacation time in order to help build the Centre. But that's missionary work; that's the Gospel. It's what we do. However, without Bishop Miller's astounding inspiration, no one would have been willing to do so. We didn't know all of the details of what we were building, but we knew it was going to be awesome; and so, we all wanted to be a part. That was a very healthy time in our church. I love projects; they have a way of pulling everyone together.

We had several people without whom we could have never built the Centre, and we owe them a huge debt of gratitude. I can't talk about everyone who assisted, but I will mention two. Along with Bishop Miller, these two faithful helpers were Tom Wiser and her grandson, Art Speck. Brother Tom is a highly skilled person—an artist, a builder, an architect, a plumber, an electrician, a cook, a mason, and the list goes on. Tom is a Army veteran who worked locally in construction, but when the need arose, he basically moved to Ghana to work at Bishop Miller's side and do whatever it took to get that Centre up and running. Tom worked through pain, and by the time he left Ghana, he was experiencing symptoms that would sadly be misdiagnosed as arthritis… but became something much more serious. Today, Tom is still our number-one overseer, our Zerubbabel. He is an amazing gift to our church and to all of our churches… while he serves from a wheelchair. He allowed himself to be pliable, and he learned to fit in to the culture, eat the food, learn the roads, and connect with many as he dutifully served in Ghana. What he accomplished was nothing short of a miracle. Besides Bishop Miller, he is the reason we have what we have. Thank you, Tom.

Then, there is Art. First of all, Art began to travel with Bishop Miller when he was quite young, as I shared in an earlier chapter. Even in her 70's, Bishop Miller tried to really "wing it" by herself, but her family and certainly each one of us were "sick" every time she left for a trip. She had suffered a few setbacks at times, and we just did not feel good about her traveling alone. She had already taken Art on some trips, and she could not see why she had to go to all the work of re-training someone else when she had already trained Art. This was a young man in his prime who began to travel the world with his grandmother. God used this time in his life to teach, train, and guide him, because He was preparing him for ministry. It was the "school of the prophets." There were others who could have gone, but I believe God allowed the bulk of this to fall on Art. Some described living and traveling with Sister Miller like "living in a pressure cooker." Art can testify that that was possibly true.

So, reluctantly at times, Art's Mom and Dad, Pastor Myrna Speck and Brother Bursie Speck, released him to go. It was not easy; he was their right-hand man at the church, and he was the baby of the family. But at the same time, Bishop Miller was Pastor Myrna's mom, and Pastor Myrna was always worried about her when she was away. Anyway, it was a major relief to everyone when Art became Bishop Miller's sidekick. When Art writes his book someday, he can share it his way; but for now, I'd like to include some of his tales within my story, so you can get a clearer view of the things that went down at that time.

Pastor Art spent massive periods of time in Ghana. He learned all about the food, the people, the customs, and the roads. Between he and Tom, they had to seek and find—with Bishop Miller tagging along—any and all of the government offices that had to do with building, tax exemption, land acquisition, shipping, NGOs (Non-Governmental Organizations), FedEX, FOREX, DSL…. Finding these in a country that had very few maps and even fewer road signs was an incredible challenge. The half has not been told! It was complicated, but they had to persevere. Bishop Miller may have been the visionary, but visionaries always need help bringing their vision to pass; and between Art and Tom—these two deserve our sincere thanks.

There is so very much that could be said about the number of people who helped, the number of flights that were taken, the amount of money we raised, and the total accumulation of who all served in Ghana, but I don't want to stray off our subject. Let's say one *huge* blanket *thank you* to everyone who had a part in the building and now in the maintenance of the Oasis International Training Centre!

Time was moving forward, and while we set many deadlines for completion, the reality was, because of the "where's" and "how's" of travel and the availability of building materials, not to mention how *long* our containers sat in the port in Tema, the dedication was held up almost a year beyond our goal. It was not complete even then, but it was getting close.

On November 25, 2000, the Oasis International Training Centre was finally dedicated. By then, we had rallied many folks to help and to attend, and Bishop Miller had made fast friends with many local pastors, leaders, and officials. The dedication would be a *huge* event. We brought a large group from Shippensburg for a very quick trip, leaving the USA on Thanksgiving night and returning the following Monday. Other friends and ministers attended from other locations of Pennsylvania as well as from our churches in Arizona and Brazil. It was a beautiful event… but the work was not finished.

In the middle of this time period, before the dedication, Pastor Art came home, proposed to Tammy, and they were married. It had to have been the quickest wedding put together *ever*! Then, at the time of the dedication, Tammy was living in Prampram with Art and was immediately thrown into some really crazy circumstances.

In the midst of all the building and construction, there was a lot of pressure. And pressure can bring misunderstandings. We had taken on a huge project and raised a lot of money; many people had sacrificed much, and at times, it began to wear on everyone. Back home, we were in a constant place of wondering who should be traveling to Ghana to help Bishop Miller. It was very trying. She was getting much older and was determined to see this through, but physically, and I hesitate to say, mentally, she was beginning to fade from us. She was not who she once was, and we understood why; but it was tough knowing how to handle the situation. She was our authority, and we didn't want to tell her what to do. But the time was quickly approaching when she needed to come home to Shippensburg.

She had already had one huge scare. On one particular trip, she returned home very sick, having developed an infection and ended up in the hospital for more than two weeks. She was very near death, but God truly used a doctor who had become a dear friend to dutifully nurse her back to health. It was a while before she went back to Ghana, but as soon as she was well enough, she was off and running again.

One time, during the height of the construction, she and Tom were sitting in the office of an official in Accra, arguing, or perhaps debating or begging, for paperwork that had been promised to us, which would further help our status as an NGO/tax-free organization. Out of nowhere, a large, heavy, wall panel fell over, landing right on Bishop Miller's head. After she recovered and was taken from the office, they were able to travel back to Prampram. Later, the official called to check on Bishop Miller and was thankful she was okay; and within days, we had our paperwork! Sometimes God's provision comes in unusual ways!

Finally, the Centre was habitable. Bishop Miller could move to the lovely apartment we had put together for her, one that would be much easier to clean and one with a little mini-kitchen. But we also needed bodies around the Centre to begin to get things rolling there, even though we had no idea what was going to roll. Eventually, adult classes were offered, and Bishop Miller was doing what she *loved.* She was surrounded by students, pastors, and leaders of churches, and she taught. She started with "Understanding God," which was the perfect study for that time, and soon, other classes were offered. But it didn't seem like we had hit the mark of the whole purpose for the Centre; and quite honestly, we had to ask, how long could Bishop Miller continue? She was approaching 90 years of age.

That was an interesting time for me. I hated that she spent so much time in Ghana, but when she was home, she became very dependent on my company. I completely understood her, although it was rough going. Her family lived far away, and I had become family. Some called me her "oxygen tank," and that was a pretty clear description. Who wants to be alone, especially as you get older? So I was her everyday companion. And it just wasn't Bishop Miller who I was helping; I also became the chauffeur service for her brother, Louie, and his wife, Helen.

I would see people my age, going here, going there; but God had assigned me to senior-citizen duty. Even so, I found myself being blessed with my assignment. Those days were very good for me, and I really enjoyed myself. We had some amazing times together. And at one point, Bishop Miller and I talked Helen and Louie into going on a cruise with us. They likewise went to Israel with us, and it was a joy to see Bishop Miller blessed, spending time with her family, which she had not previously had time to do. She kept telling everyone that she was semi-retired. What a joke! Her semi-retired status could actually be equated with some young person's full-time job with overtime! She was truly a go-getter.

But as the days passed, Bishop Miller started to feel the pressure of all she was doing, and her age was truly having a serious effect on her in many ways. I know that she knew it, but she was pretty good at hiding it—although her memory caused her to do and say some *very* uncharacteristic things. But to me—this was not Bishop Miller.

I remember hearing of one day when Sister Miller was faithfully teaching "Understanding God" in the upstairs assembly room in the Training Centre in Ghana. All of a sudden, she stopped speaking, blacked out, and fell unconscious to the floor. The class then began to pray and command life to flow through her body. And she awoke. She was then carried to her apartment, and Diane, who was with her at the time, was sworn to secrecy. We knew *nothing* about this episode until Bishop Miller began to recover. We never heard what took place, but we know it had to be an attack of the enemy. But it didn't work. Only in God's time would she leave this earth.

With her persuasion, her doctor from the States visited the Centre in Ghana. After he returned home, he asked me to come see him and frankly told me that we needed to do whatever it took to get her to come home. Believe me, we were working on it.

During those days, Pastor Art had moved back home with Tammy, and they now had a baby daughter, Elizabeth. So, naturally, he needed to stay home for longer periods of time. I have to give it to them, their honeymoon was actually spent in Prampram, and they lived there for awhile before they went home to stay, more or less, permanently. I think they should have named their daughter Prampram!

Our predicament was figuring out… who? Who should be there in Ghana? We could not leave Bishop Miller alone, so the lot naturally fell on anyone who was not employed full-time. The Centre was like a revolving door. People were coming and going, going and coming, and it had to be the right fit. In all honesty, though, no one actually felt a call to go there. It was a never-ending pressure, and for me, I lived in guilt. I sometimes thought I was to just pack up and go, but I didn't want to be there alone. And I could not be there, just with Bishop Miller. Some local lady pastors would stay with her at times, and we tried hiring someone to assist her… but nothing seemed to work. It truly had to be a calling. God had to call your number. And something told me that He had not called mine.

During that time, three people became a part of the comings and goings at the Centre—Diane McKee and Ambrose and Susanne Brennan. Diane was a full-time teacher from the Huntingdon Oasis, and Ambrose and Sue worked full-time at our church. Sue was our secretary, a leader with the children, and basically an all-around, amazingly talented woman. In my mind, she could do anything. Ambrose, her husband, was an accountant, worked in IT, and was one of those "Jack of all Trades, Master of A Lot" people. He served as youth leader and teacher. And to be honest, in my mind, he could do anything too!

Sister Diane was an elder at the church in Huntingdon and was also amazingly talented. She *loved* to teach, and still does. To her, it is *not* just a job; it truly is who she is. All you have to do is be around her, and it oozes out of her.

Without any planning on our part, God placed Diane, Susie, and Ambrose together at the Training Centre, and eventually through a true "trial by fire of the Holy Spirit" for each of them, it was obvious to everyone that God had indeed called their number. The hardest thing ever for me was to admit to myself that God was calling Sue and Ambrose away for a time. Even so, I did begin to admit it and knew it was going to happen. I think I actually accepted it even before they did. At first, I didn't think I could run the church here without their help. They had been my right hand and my everything. Over the years, they showed great empathy and love for me, which was beyond just friendship, and they had become my family. I loved their kids, and I loved them.

But the writing was on the wall, and in time, they saw the writing as well. Whether they ever really *felt* "the call" or not, I doubt. Sometimes that experience is overrated. Sometimes, you just move in obedience, and amazingly later, you suddenly realize that the only way you can be doing what you are doing is to have been called to do so. Sue and Ambrose moved to Ghana when their son was still in high school and their daughter was in college. This was tough for everyone, but it was also imperative that Bishop Miller be relieved of her duties… and soon.

Her 90th birthday had come, and we planned to do it up right. We rented a hotel in Accra and sent out formal invitations. I, along with some others, packed our bags, and we journeyed to Africa to join the party… and we hoped to also bring Bishop Miller home.

The party was a huge success, and the following day, we held an Open House at the Centre, which was now finished, and furnished, and ready for tours. It also gave us another opportunity to celebrate her birthday. It was another lovely event. Then the next day, Art was to leave, and following him, I was to leave with Pastor Myrna and Bishop Miller. Bishop Miller already had her ticket, but during the last few hours, she began to dig her heels in and say she was not going home. I used every tactic to get her on that plane. Finally, when we heard that her brother was not well, that seemed to be the ticket. She was packed and ready to go home to be at his side.

We said a very tearful goodbye to Susie, then Ambrose drove us to Accra, and we decided to shop and have dinner on the way. While at dinner, I received the call that Bishop Miller's brother, Louie, had died, and I made the decision to not tell her until we were halfway across the Atlantic. And this would be her last trip across the ocean from her beloved Africa. Her work there was done; and someone else would pick up the vision.

That's the wonderful thing about a vision. We see it through our eyes for a time, and we can do as much with it ourselves as we know; but often, God allows us to pass it on to another, to whom He will make the vision even clearer. Bishop Miller's great joy was seeing someone do something better than she could do it. She wanted you to fly higher, jump further, and run faster than she could. That's the sign of a true leader. She was not doing it for herself; she was doing what she did for the advancement of the Kingdom of the Lord Jesus Christ. And what she did, she always did with everything she had in her.

The sign leading into Prampram

The Sealane Hotel, where I communed with a scorpion

The Sealane Hotel

The Annex

Ben and Salome Kusah with Bishop Miller

The Oasis International Training Centre

Tom Wiser on the roof of the Centre

Bishop Miller, Art and myself in Ghana

Bishop Miller cuts the ribbon at the dedication

Ambrose and Susanne Brennan

Diane Mckee

Three amazing servants of God in Ghana

Chapter Thirteen

UP AND RUNNING—AT HOME AND ABROAD

Your sun shall no longer go down, nor shall your moon withdraw itself; for the Lord will be your everlasting light, and the days of your mourning shall be ended. Also your people shall all be righteous; They shall inherit the land forever, the branch of My planting, the work of My hands, that I may be glorified. A little one shall become a thousand, and a small one a strong nation. I, the Lord, will hasten it in its time.
(Isaiah 60:20-22 NKJV)

Serving the Lord Jesus Christ is a blast! You never know what is going to happen next, and when you have a leader who is creative, innovative, and a Holy-Ghost spitfire, things never slow down, or do they?

Bishop Miller had left the Centre in able hands, and now, she was happily home from Ghana. The full picture of what the Centre would become was still unclear, but at least there was an important commitment from Ambrose and Susanne Brennan, and soon, Sister Diane McKee would join them. With that team in place, along with Pastor Art's guidance and Bishop Miller's direction, in time a plan would emerge.

When Bishop Miller returned to the States, the first thing she had to deal with was her Brother Louie's funeral. I found it odd that she asked me to plan most of it. I did, and of course, his loving sister, Elvina spoke. After those days, Bishop Miller seemed to be in a little bit of a slump, but after what she had just accomplished in Ghana, it was no wonder. She preached every now and then, but at this point in her life and ministry, she had pretty much put her trust in me to "run the show." It was frightening to preach in front of her, but the more I did, the more she encouraged me, said "Amen," and cheered me on. During this growing time, I gained an important confidence that I truly needed. I guess I could say, it was good to know that she trusted me to handle God's Word.

Also during this time, it became obvious that Sister Miller was beginning to forget things, and she was sleeping more than I remember her doing. I found that I was constantly reminding her of things, and in time, it became somewhat irritating. But I did all I could to keep her moving.

One day, I was planning a trip to a local store called "Tuesday Morning," and I enticed her to go along. It was good just to get her out of the building. When we got into the car and she asked where we were headed, I replied, "We're going to Tuesday Morning." Then we started to travel down the highway, and by the time we had reached our exit, she had probably asked me about seven or eight times, "Where did you say we were going?" Each time that I replied, I put an extra emphasis on my answer to help her remember that we were indeed going to "Tuesday Morning." When we were about one turn away from the store, once again, she looked up at me and asked, "Nancy, where did you say we were going?" I looked over at her with a smile on my face, hesitated, then together we said, "TUESDAY MORNING!" What did we do next? We laughed and laughed and laughed; and we both knew why we were laughing. That was one of our last full-fledged shopping trips together, and I'll never forget that day.

At other times, when Sue and Ambrose would call from Ghana to talk with her or when they would come home and show her pictures of the Centre, incredibly, those pictures sparked little or no memory for her. It was sad and unbelievable. Then, after a few more years at home, she was not regularly getting up for church, and if I woke her, it seemed she didn't know it was Sunday... and I really hated to keep bugging her. It's not like she was going to backslide if she missed church. She would gently ask me to take the service, which I was already planning to do, but these days were difficult for all of us.

One morning sitting at her breakfast table, we were talking... and it was just small talk... when she looked up at me and said, "Nancy, I know what I want to say, but I can't say it." We shed some tears together that day. I took her hand, and I assured her that she didn't have to worry; we would carry on. We would do the talking for her. Looking back in my presbytery, God spoke that I would be a repeater of her words.

About five years after returning from Africa, Bishop Miller was no longer able to come to church, and she stayed inside most of the time. Even the suggestion of a shopping trip could not get her outside, but I still managed to take her for a few drive-through meals at Sonic from time to time. She loved riding in my red VW bug, and those trips seemed to perk her up, if only for a short while.

She was leaving us, ever so slowly, but maybe God allowed this gradual change so we could possibly get used to the idea that she would not be with us forever. It was hard for me to imagine losing my mentor, my best friend, my pastor. I would say that I had ventured into a state of denial during this time. I was trying to do all I could to bring her back, if that was possible. Remember, I was her "oxygen tank." I was non-stop, making her favorite foods, but even that did little to spark her. Nothing seemed to taste right.

My emotions were a bit raw; I didn't want to lose her. For all the times that, in my heart, I may have been tired of her instruction, her guidance, and her "mothering"; now I yearned for it to never end. It was possible that the intimate talks, the uproarious moments of laughter, and the heady times of Bible study together would be no more, and I was anxious, sad, impatient, and a tiny bit depressed. I cried a lot, took every word she said seriously... even though some of her words were simply not the way she would have talked to anyone, let alone me. I have never been a caregiver for anyone, except Sister Miller's dogs, and this was not how I wanted our last days together to be.

Add to this circumstance, a predicament in one of our sister churches that needed a strong hand, and there was no one who could deliver the hand of correction. Bishop Miller was somewhat "down for the count"; I was not in a position of that type of authority; and our other leaders did not know which way to turn. Unfortunately, the enemy took advantage of this lapse of leadership, and the problem only escalated. That's when you know if people are true blue. You never hit someone when they are down, but we all felt truly hit and bruised from it. All of this happened at the worst possible time.

Of course, all the way around, we continued to bow our knees before God concerning every part of these intense times. When you walk through pain or suffering, you know that God knows, and the reassurance in His presence did wonders for everyone. But being in the position I was in, I must admit that it took a toll on me physically and spiritually. I could not see the light at the end of the tunnel, and I was weakening. If it would not have been for those who consistently lifted my hands, I'm not sure where I would have ended up myself. But this experience showed me a vivid picture of the Body of Christ and how much we need each other. Oh, do we need each other!

In 2012, Bishop Miller moved permanently to an elder care facility, where she lived out the rest of her days. Thankfully at that time, we could joyfully visit her, eat with her, pray for her, sing to her, and minister to her without the burden of her physical care and the struggle that it sometimes involved. During those four years and four months, as she slowly ebbed away, many people from her past and those with whom she had ministered alongside from all over the world made the trip to see her and sat once again beside her, to honor her and thank her for her impartation into their lives. They came even when she was unable to respond anymore. It was a joyous, but somber time. This time also afforded anyone in our church who had not done so, time to sit with her, talk to her, cry, pray, and love her for one last time.

This period also gave me a huge chunk of time to heal, to reflect, and to come to grips with my calling, which to this day I have not let go of. As I served this great saint of God, she poured her life into me. The fruit that is manifested in me and through me today is nothing short of a miracle, considering I was the "little hippie girl" who found her way to Deliverance Temple to help Sister Miller. But, again, she was the one who helped me! I stand amazed, as I see prophetic words that were spoken over me come to pass and witness how God is fulfilling what Bishop Miller always believed I would accomplish.

During the last years of her life, I wept as I poured out my love to her, and looking into her eyes, I thanked her again and again for every word, every correction, every trip, every time she helped me. It seemed I couldn't say it enough.

I reflected what God had spoken to me, way back in 1974.

I can still hear those words—"Help her." God told me to "Help her."

On August 2, 2016, Bishop Elvina E. Miller was ushered into glory. Her work here was done, she had finished her course. With a new body that would last for all eternity, she would once again dance before her Lord Jesus. Gone from this earth, she is home.

It has been an honor to serve Bishop Miller, and my prayer is this, "Lord Jesus, may each word I say be measured by Your Word. May the decisions I make reflect Your love for this world. And may the group of believers You have entrusted to us always know of a little Italian lady, who gave it all, who spent herself for the Gospel, and who lived as an example every moment I knew her. God, may I follow her, as she followed You."

What a legacy!

What a life!

What a lady!

Bishop Miller on the phone, talking to the staff in Ghana

Bishop Miller, right before she left to come home from Ghana

Bishop Miller on her porch in Shippensburg

Spiritual Mother and Daughter

Bishop Miller, Holly, Andrea, and Natalie Crawford

Addendum One

COUNTRIES IN WHICH BISHOP ELVINA E. MILLER HAS MINISTERED

Argentina
Australia
Austria
Bolivia
Brazil
British Virgin Islands
Canada
Chile
China
Columbia
Costa Rica
Cuba
Cyprus
Dominican Republic

Gambia
Germany
Ghana
Greece
Guatemala
Hong Kong
India
Israel
Italy
Ivory Coast
Japan
Kenya
Malawi
Mali
Mauritius

Mexico
Nigeria
Panama
Portugal
Puerto Rico
Russia
South Africa
South Korea
Spain
United Kingdom
United States of America
Virgin Islands
Zambia
Zimbabwe

Addendum Two

FAUNA*

Bishop Miller loved animals. *Loved* animals! She tried to bring a monkey home from Brazil, but when someone found out it was "endangered," that ended that! In Shippensburg, however, because of her love for animals, we have made a home for cats, doves, finches, fish, and now dogs. While my original intent was to include this section as a chapter in the main body of the book, with wise counsel (thanks, Lyle!) I have added this rather large section as an addendum. I hope you enjoy the additional lessons and joy we have had as we have certainly become a "sanctuary city for dogs."

"If reincarnation exists, I want to come back as a Temple dog."
Denny Cook

Good people are good to their animals; the "good-hearted" bad people kick and abuse them.
Proverbs 12:10 MSG

Yep, Sister Miller *loved* animals. If she would have truly had her way, our church would have had a zebra in the backyard, cows and horses in the fields, monkeys in cages, and a literal bird sanctuary contained within our walls. But in thinking this through, I could not conclude this book without a section dedicated to the number of dogs and the countless lessons we all learned as we played host and caretaker over the years to some amazingly, wonderful fur-people (or Temple dogs) who lived in our church.

Let's take this trip chronologically, that is, if we can actually remember who came when!

Honey Bun

Somehow, I recalled that the first dog, Honey Bun, was given as a gift to Sister and Brother Miller from June and Arlene Stitzel. June and Arlene, long-time members of the church, gifted this snippy little poodle to the Millers, and soon it became part of the family. I arrived near the end of his life, when training had long since flown out the door and this little, white, curly-haired dog was *beyond* spoiled rotten.

After Brother Miller passed away, Honey Bun's care fell on those who could help out when Bishop Miller went on mission trips, and eventually, because I was around, the responsibility fell on me. I am not sure why, but this dog liked me… the feeling was not mutual! Honey Bun would go into depression when Sister Miller would begin to pack, and after she left, he would go on hunger strikes and hide when it was time to go "atta-boy."

Sister Miller often times would want Honey Bun to stay in her apartment while she was away at night, so he would feel comfortable. The only problem was, the Millers had a king-sized bed, and he would position himself under the bed exactly in the middle where we had to crawl and with "cookies," *beg* him to come out from under the bed. But that wasn't the only problem. If you did manage to grab his collar, he had a ferocious bite! The only way to capture him while also saving yourself from losing a finger was to throw a blanket over his head and then grab him.

This predicament was really beginning to work on me. He wasn't my dog, and I could not have cared less! But I began to notice that Honey Bun started to come to me and would sit under my chair during church. One time, when Bishop Miller was on an extended trip, Honey Bun sat whimpering at my feet, and when he looked up into my eyes, I was smitten. This dear little animal had lost his daddy, Brother Miller, and now his mommy was away, too. I reached down, picked him up, snuggled with him, and realized, just like many of us at various times, he simply needed a hug. After that, my snotty "I couldn't care less" attitude was gone. Plus, I had come to realize that part of the "help her" might also include caring for her animals. Later that summer, Honey Bun went to doggie heaven. I remember feeling really bad for Bishop Miller, but I didn't shed any tears myself. I liked the dog by that time, but wasn't as attached to him as she was. Goodbye, Honey Bun.

Libby

As time marched on, there was no more Honey Bun, and I was just as glad. I had accumulated responsibilities and never felt like I had enough time for "poor, little, ole' me," and naturally, I didn't want another dog. *But,* one day, in came Ward Wiser, who was the "daddy" to several poodles, and in the pocket of his work shirt was this little black and white (Parti) miniature poodle. He announced in front of a group of women that this dog was the runt of the litter, and he couldn't find anyone to take her. So, if we didn't want her, he would just dispose of her. Guess what? That would have never happened! Every woman in that room screamed, except me, because I could see the writing on the wall. That little, innocent dog would be one more "thing" that I would have to do, and I was not interested. And another prissy poodle at that!

Of course, you know what happened. Sister Miller gently grabbed that little dog, and she was ours. Ward told us she was born on July 4th, so her name had to be Liberty or Libby. Everyone agreed, and I had a new ward. One of the other girls who lived at the church was enamoured with this "ball of fur," and she immediately took charge. I couldn't have been happier, *but* for some strange reason, this dog did not take to her. You guessed it—she was Sister Miller's dog, but she was in love with me. Aaaand, it didn't take long until I was in love with her.

If anyone thought Honey Bun was spoiled, they soon discovered that he didn't hold a candle to this little dog. Libby was truly "the church mascot." She was a beautiful Parti color and was a dear, friendly, loving dog. She hardly ever had to walk, because she was carried everywhere, and she slept on someone's lap in every service. Twice, one of her legs was broken, because her little body always got under someone's feet. Yet this endeared her even more to each of us. But she was *bad*! With Libby, no matter what she did, she got away with it. I was in love, and I learned that when you love something, you will do anything for that something. It's called unconditional love.

Libby lived to be around 13 years old. The last three years of her life, she developed diabetes, and Nurse Nancy had to test her urine every day, calculate her insulin, and then give her a shot every morning. When she began to decline, we took her to the vet. Amber went with me, and we both wept as we petted that beautiful little dog goodbye. Later that night, the vet called to tell us she had passed.

By the time little Libby had developed diabetes and also went blind, she was being carried gently up and down the steps by big, strong football players and five-year-old kids. She was loved on by many, and for some, she was the first pet they had ever had. When the vet called us during our Sunday night service to tell us she had passed, it was a sad night. And even though we had a guest speaker, everyone sitting in the service was crying. He probably thought we were out of our minds.

As my custom was every night before bed, I would walk up to the sanctuary, check the doors, and say goodnight to Sister Miller. That night when I went into the sanctuary, I heard the sound of someone crying. It was dark, and I couldn't see. So I said, "Who's there?" Out of the darkness a familiar voice answered, "Bubba." I said, "Bubba, what's wrong?" Across the sanctuary he said, "Libby." Yep, she affected us all. She was the perfect, little dog.

But from that time on, I knew we would probably never be without a dog… or two… or three living in our church.

Holly

When Sister Miller realized how many people were in the "depths of despair" over the passing of one little dog (and she was majorly upset, too), she made a firm declaration. "We will never get another dog," she said. Then she added that everyone was too upset by the death of this little doggie, and it disrupted the whole church. I kept my mouth shut. I too was so heartbroken over Libby, and I decided to use "mind over matter" to help me believe that I could handle life without a dog.

Mary Lou, my roommate, on the other hand, was adamant that we should have another dog, and she continued to assail Sister Miller almost daily about how much a dog makes a house a home. I just silently prayed. I was truly sad. I'm a dog lover at heart, and it wasn't going to change. And I knew God could do a miracle. Hey, even God changed His mind a few times!

Lo and behold, one day, Mary Lou came home from working at the bank with a skip in her step. After dinner, she summoned me to her room to show me why. There, she produced two pictures of this adorable, scruffy dog, and she began to tell me about her. That day, she had been assigned to visit and do the paperwork on a loan for a young, married woman who had been in a near fatal accident. What greeted her at the door and would not let her alone, was Bunky, a four-month-old Cairn Terrier. I was already in love, because all of my life I had wanted a real live Toto—this had to be God!

I don't know whether it was Mary Lou's continuous nagging or God's mercy, but when she approached Sister Miller with the "tail" about this dear, little, friendly dog that we could have for *free*, Sister Miller said, "Oh, alright." We were overjoyed! We were delirious! And I immediately knew that this little dog was an answer to my prayers. Of course, she would be our responsibility—Mary Lou had already claimed her as her own, but was willing to share. So, the time was set, and Bunky was to come for a visit to say "Hi." If we liked her, she would be ours.

Well, Sunday couldn't come soon enough, and when the doorbell rang, a gang of girls in the Court Room of the church working on some task received the owner, and in came Bunky. From the very beginning, she was a pistol! She must have done 25 laps around that room, as we all sat on the floor. Mary Lou tried to entice her to sit on her lap, but Bunky would only run to me, kiss me on the face, and sit squarely on my lap, and then kiss me all over again. It was love at first sight! Yep, like it or not, Mary Lou, this dog had picked me. I was her mommy.

I immediately renamed her Holly after my best friend in high school, and we had our dog. Of course, Bishop Miller had given us some hard and fast rules. The dog could not leave our apartment when anyone was in the church, and that was final.

Well, Holly was around for about two weeks when I noticed she was no longer interested in food. She seemed peppy enough, but she would not eat. Then she seemed to lose all of her energy. I called our vet and reported the symptoms, and he gave me some ideas as to what to do to get her to eat, which worked for about one meal… but that was it. The next Saturday night, in the middle of the night, Holly woke me—she had gotten sick *everywhere*. I knew something was really wrong. I tried to nurse her through the night, but by morning, I called our vet and he asked us bring her to him immediately. By the time of the trip, she also had diarrhea. It was awful… and I was a mess! Was this a "the Lord giveth, and the Lord taketh away" thing?

The vet kept her so that he could observe her for a while, and then called after church that day to tell me the dire diagnosis. She had Parvo Virus. She had been housed in a kennel and most likely picked it up from another dog… and was too young to vaccinate for it. If she had a will to live, she would have a long battle, but the vet thought she might make it. At the time, though, she just laid in the cage. The doctor had attached two IV's to her; one was nutrition, the other was medicine. By Monday, she was no better. Tuesday, she was worse. I was sick, and Bishop Miller was very upset. She thought, *"Here we go again."* But I was about to learn an amazing lesson on mothering.

Thursday morning, Dr. Fague called me and said, "She's no better; she's no worse. But I have a thought." He continued, "Do you have an old coat you can throw away? And do you have something that's yours with your scent?" I answered, "Yes, my pj's, and yes, I have an old nylon coat."

119

He ended the call by saying "Bring them and come in today around 3:00 p.m." I showed up promptly at 3:00 p.m., and Dr. Fague explained, "Holly is so young, she needs a reason to live; you need to be that reason. These dogs really love people, and she needs you right now." He then said, "Every afternoon, I want you to come in here, and I'll get you a chair. I want you to hold her and talk to her for about an hour every day, that is, if you have time. I'll put your pj's in her cage so she doesn't forget you, and she can sleep on them."

By the time this "experiment" would be over, I realized that my coat would be ready to throw out and so would my pj's, because Holly had no control over her bodily functions and she smelled *bad*! Even so, every day between 2:00 or 3:00 in the afternoon, I would take my stinky coat out of the plastic bag in the trunk of the car, put it on, and hold our very sick puppy. I would talk to her, and I would pray for her. I asked God a thousand times to please not let her die. Then each morning, this kind doctor would call me with a report. It felt good to know she had lived through the night. For two weeks plus, I held that dear, skinny dog and told her how much I loved her and continued to believe God. I was so thankful Bishop Miller put up with this. She was equally as upset but she could have never put up with that smell. She did go with me one time to see her, but she sat with Dr. Fague while I held Holly.

Seemingly, there was no change, as far as I could see. But Dr. Fague did say that if she made it two weeks and didn't get diarrhea again, there was a good chance she would live. But then we had to be concerned about the state of her digestive system. She was seriously sick.

It was a Sunday morning, of course, and the phone rang at 6:00 a.m. It was Dr. Fague, and I braced myself for the news that Holly had died. Dr. Fague said, in only the way that a wonderful, loving old vet would say, "Well, my wife woke me up this morning at 4:00 a.m. because she couldn't sleep. She said there was a dog in obvious distress that had been barking non-stop. I went downstairs, and I looked in at the dogs. Everyone was fine, then I went into Holly's room. There she was standing on her feet, barking with the most pathetic sounding bark I had ever heard. So I gave her a tiny bit of water, but then she got mad at me and barked all the more. I said to myself, "I think she's hungry!" So I gave her a half teaspoon of wet food, and she gulped it down. Then she barked more, so I waited and gave her another half teaspoon. She still was not satisfied, so every half hour since then, I've been giving her a little more." He said, "Nancy, I think you have your Christmas miracle; I think she's beaten it."

I bawled! One and a half weeks later, on New Year's Eve, we brought Holly home. Aunt Cheryl held her all night in the kitchen, and every other hour, she would feed her. Holly had laid in that hospital for four and one-half weeks until she had been ready to come home. Now, all she needed was to put meat back on her bones and we had our Holly back!

I found it hard to throw that coat away. There was something about remembering the dire straits she was in, and that smell that reminded me of the whole ordeal. It was like a scar from a lifesaving surgery—one that helps you remember where you once were. That was precisely what Bishop Miller had done for me. In my "stinky, sick stage" she hadn't been afraid to get next to me and help me find healing. She saw what could be, rather than what was. I ended up washing and rewashing the jacket, and when it finally fell into rags years later, I got rid of it. Right now, I can still see it in my mind's eye.

But that's not the end of Holly's story. She was around nine months old, and her papers from the breeder had not come as I was told that they would. We had submitted all the right information, and so I began to backtrack. The person she came from didn't know where the papers were. The pet store where she was purchased didn't know where they were. I learned that the breeder was located in Fredrick, Maryland, so I got her number and called her. We began to talk, and I explained the reason for the call. After a short conversation, she asked where the dog was living and who the owners were. I said, "It's kind of hard to understand, but she lives in a church; she's the church dog." With that, the breeder began to laugh and said, "Let me tell you a story."

She continued, "A little while back, I was trying to breed my dog, but she would not conceive. We had all but given up, when one night we hosted a prophet who came to speak at our church. He thanked us for the meal, and before he left he asked us if there was anything he could believe God with us for. I said, 'Well, yes, but it's a little unusual. We are trying to breed our dog, but she will not conceive. Could you pray that she gets pregnant?'

"So the minister leaned down, laid hands on our little dog, and prayed for her. Then he said, 'She will get pregnant, and every dog in that litter will be involved in the ministry or will be owned by a minister.' "

She concluded the story by saying, "All the puppies ended up in ministers' and missionaries' homes, and this is the only one I didn't know about. So where do you live?"

I shared that we lived in Shippensburg.

She then asked, "Is your pastor a short Italian woman?"

I answered, "Yes, she is. Her name is Sister Miller."

The breeder owner laughed again and said, "The prophet talked about your church and her the entire evening when he was here."

I said, "Was his name Tim Myer?"

"Yes," she said, and we both laughed. Tim and his wife, Esther, were dear friends; this was no coincidence!

Holly could not have died! She was ordained to be our dog, and she ended up providing hours and hours of "ministry" to Sister Miller and to everyone in the church. She was, indeed, again, our church mascot. When she came to the services, her habit was to bark at the door. The ushers would then jump up, open the door, and she would walk in, jump on a chair, and go to sleep. Holly lived to be more than 16 years old. She sat at Bishop's feet, slept with her, and rode the UPS truck. She was a perfect dog... and she was absolutely so smart. She provided hours of entertainment for our kids growing up, and she paved the way for other Cairn Terriers that we would own. Long live, Holly! There was no "fur-person" like her.

Vinee

I can't remember the timing, but Bishop Miller and I were out for a drive when I decided to stop at the pet store to buy some food for Holly. Bishop Miller had *always* wanted a Chow Chow. She knew nothing about them except that they were beautiful, and at this time, she wouldn't rest until she got one... and was always on the hunt. On that fateful day, I just happened to look in the cages at the store, and there she was—a three-month-old Chow. Oh my goodness, was she beautiful! I got back in the car, and I didn't want to be deceptive, so I told her. That afternoon, yes, we drove home with a Chow Chow.

Of course, everyone loved her. She was gorgeous, and once again, she became my dog. But when Bishop Miller realized how much she was going to shed, she *really* became my dog. But I had no idea how to raise a dog with that strong of a will. Vinee had about seven good years when she began to get very protective of me and very territorial. She snapped at several people, growled at a bunch of others, and then the hammer came down when she bit two people in the church. We sequestered her to the back hallway, and she continued to have a close network of friends until... we firmly believe she was protecting me... she bit Bishop Miller.

Bishop Miller did not understand that Vinee had no peripheral vision, and she often would attempt to pet her from behind, which would always scare Vinee. But the writing was on the wall. One afternoon, we came in from a shopping trip, and Vinee literally went after Bishop Miller. I was scared to death. I was beginning to be afraid of her biting someone else, and some people were afraid of her even though they had no cause; they were just afraid. But it made me nervous, and Vinee was nervous too. So I made the call; she had to be put down. We didn't want to, but there was nothing we could do.

This absolutely beautiful dog, the most luscious Chow Chow I had ever seen, knew she had crossed the line. After her attack on Bishop Miller, she laid down in the corner of my office, knowing that everyone was upset, and she was the cause. The next day would be *the* day, and that day, I lay on the bed with her until 2:30 p.m. I cried, she gave me bite kisses, people came to say goodbye, and then sadly, Vinee went to doggie heaven.

What did I learn? Well… what did we all learn? You don't bite off more than you can chew. Bad word choice, maybe? We didn't have the experience to raise a strong-willed dog like a Chow. Those dogs are for people who can train them and properly socialize them. Just because you can have one, doesn't mean you should. It also helped me to know that some things are just not a good idea and sometimes I had to be the one to put my foot down.

In Vinee's defense, she loved her caretakers. She loved me, Ambrose, Aunt Cheryl, and a few others; and she was in love with Johanne Thompson. Sister Johanne was not even a dog person, but Vinee had her so trained. Johanne gave her many cookies while she sat and typed in the office every day. Good bye, beautiful dog!

Harrison

While Holly was still doing well, a new family began to come to our church, who had a Cairn Terrier. Bubba, Josh, and Jeremy lived on Walnut Street, and they had already purchased a dog that was somehow related to this new family's little Cairn. His name was Frodo. It was at this time that we began to think that Holly might need a companion. She had several (which I'll talk about later), but we needed one to live right in the building with her. This new family was intending to breed their dog, and when the time came, their dog had three adorable Cairn Terriers. It just so happened that the mother of the family was a hair stylist, and each week, Bishop Miller would go to their home to get her hair done. Every day while she waited, they would place Harrison on her lap. After two weeks, it was a done deal. And in late June, right before the Creation Festival, we had a new dog. *Great* timing! The mother dog had rejected the puppy, so she had barely been weaned. And he was already so spoiled that training him was a riot!

He absolutely refused to walk on a leash and cried non-stop, so I would have to pick him up and drag him on the leash until he *decided* to stand. Every "atta boy" time was an adventure. But in due time, Harry became our little "lover boy." While spoiled beyond belief, little Harry, who at this writing, is almost 12 years old, has been a wonderful dog.

Although he is literally afraid of everything, he has become a great dog. He gets along with most people, but he always needs a proper introduction with gobs of cookies, so that he can "get to know you." Harry's place in our history is unique—he was Bishop Miller's loving companion during her final days living here, and dear little Harrison was actually part of the tell-tale sign that our Bishop needed more care than we could provide anymore. She didn't mistreat him, but without going into details, we knew she was not herself because we had to eventually take him away from her. It was tough on Harry and tough on us. Harry is still the "man of the house" and has really seen some stuff in his days at our church.

Lucy

When Vinee went to doggy heaven, I was a mess. Oh, I wasn't hysterical, but there was a flow of tears off and on, and I could barely talk about it. I *loved* that dog. One day, I was taking Bishop Miller to the bank and out of the blue she said, "What I think you should do, is get another dog like Holly." Good goga booga! That was all I needed to hear, and I was on the search. However this time, I was searching for a brindle Cairn Terrier, so we could have a real Toto.

I called breeders everywhere, then resorted to a pet store where we eventually found little Lucy. From the very beginning, she was mine. I was the only one who could pick her up without a struggle. But once again, this breed did not fail… she was a beautiful, loving, and smart dog. She could do tons of tricks and was so very friendly, but a little over-skittish. She and Harry were buddies—real buddies. It was a good thing she was "fixed" or we would have had litters of little Cairns running around! We sometime regretted it; she was such a darling dog.

Again, I loved this little creature.

On another day. Patti took her out for a walk and halfway around the one sidewalk, Lucy had a seizure. After a few minutes, and with George even doing mouth to snout CPR on her, she died. She was only five years old. Ed and Nancy were away, Sue and Ambrose were in Africa, Bishop Miller wasn't doing so well at that time, and I was devastated. My Lucy… my Lucy, who was named after Lucy in the Chronicles of Narnia, was dead. So sudden… and a very sad day.

While we called everyone in the church, Cheryl picked her up and made a little bed for her in the Court Room. And then we had a "public viewing" for her that day. Yes, we are crazy. Harry lay beside her all afternoon, and finally, we wrapped her up, and the guys put her in the freezer. They had a plan. Sam Wiser, Sr. was already making a little mini casket, so we could properly bury this little girl the next day. Then on Sunday afternoon, we gathered at her gravesite, lowered her in the ground, and covered her up. We said a few words, threw flowers over her grave, and then we all cracked up. We knew we were ridiculous!

What was wrong with us? Actually, nothing! They knew she was my baby, and this simple act of kindness toward me over the sudden death of my beloved dog was a true act of love on display, the way only people who are family would do. At that time period, emotionally, we were walking through Bishop Miller's somewhat downward spiral, and somehow, this gesture of love for me, helped, as silly as it sounds. That was the story of Lucy.

Tundra

My memories of Tundra are hazy. She was Kevin's dog. I remember going to see her; she was a beautiful white German Shepard who lived outside in our "dog run," which I disapproved of. I don't believe dogs should be outside, but that's just me. Kevin was in charge of Tundra, and she lived during Holly's reign. In fact, we have pictures of them playing together as pups. My most prominent memory of Tundra was that Bishop Miller once told Kevin that if he couldn't take care of a dog, he couldn't take care of a wife.

Tundra died early—we believe she suffered from a situation in her stomach after she ate bones given to her, which she probably should not have had. Bye, bye, Tundra!

Rex

Rex was a German Shepard that was Rene's dog. Rex was a beautiful dog. I didn't have that much contact with him, because I was afraid of him. He had a mean growl, but as I recall, he was aggressive only one time—when he backed us down the steps and into the kitchen growling the whole way!

I guess it was just because I didn't know him, that I was afraid of him. Rene loved Rex, and Rex loved Rene. Then Rex got sick and died young as a result of cancer. He withered away to practically nothing, and on the day that we took him to the vet, in order to save him from the pain he was in, and to go to doggie heaven, I could not stop crying again. Rex licked my hand, and I regretted that I had not given him more of a chance. He looked at me through his beautiful eyes, and you could tell he was suffering. He was Rene's best buddy, and I loved Rene; he was one of my best friends, and my heart ached for him. It's like that with friends. When they hurt, you hurt. Goodbye, Rexroth Rene Posey!

Chow and Lizzie

These two dogs were such cool dogs. Chow was a Chow Chow/Lab mix that had zero Chow characteristics, except a purple tongue, and Lizzie was a full-bred Black Lab. These two girls lived outside as well as in the Educational Building, and together they wreaked havoc, ate people's sandwiches, inhaled pounds and pounds of food that was not theirs, controlled the rabbit population, and were fabulous companions to countless kids and adults through their long lives. They were infamous! We got Chow from the Humane Society after Bishop Miller saw her at the nursing home and decided we needed another "outside" dog to protect us. That was a joke. Chow wouldn't hurt a flea, and Lizzy was even worse. Talk about spoiled! All they wanted to do was to be retrievers and eat… and that's about all they did, besides give countless hours of love to the multitudes.

Lizzie was named after Bishop Miller (her middle name) and was actually related to Bishop Miller. She was one of the pups from her grandson, Rod and his wife, Carol's dog. She was a beauty, but suffered with hip problems throughout her life. Those two dogs had balls all over the field, and Chow especially could jam several tennis balls into her mouth at once.

One of the many things Ambrose did was to help take care of the dogs at the church. But when Ambrose went away to Africa, their care got complicated. It was hard to have two big dogs with just ladies to care for them. They were both getting older and needed to be walked every day. It was tough. Eventually, they both passed away, but not before performing a very important task in Ambrose's life.

Before Ambrose was called full-time to go to Africa, he had a few situations and personal struggles that he was working through. He had already been in Africa and had come home, and from the way it sounded, he was not going back. I was "in charge" during the day, and there was really nothing I could do to help him, which I could see. He was not involved in ministry during that time; every day, he would stop over to see if there was anything he could do. After we would sit, talk, cry, and pray together, several times a day, he would walk Chow and Lizzie. Ambrose credits those two crazy labs with an amazing time of great healing in his life. I think he shed more tears when they died than anyone. Through them, he learned a simple obedience and humbling, which is why today he serves as the Head Administrator over our whole operation in Ghana.

While Chow and Lizzie lived, they took part in a continuous path of destructive behavior with regard to the theft of food in the Educational Building. We still do not know *how* it happened, and we didn't know who to blame. But somehow those dogs would get into the kitchen, eat anything within their reach, and leave the evidence everywhere. It was getting pretty irritating, but was also hilarious. We kind of always suspected Lizzie, so she got a good deal of the blame. But it wasn't her. The minute Chow passed away, the pillaging stopped. After that, I made it a conscious effort to make everyone apologize to poor Liz for the years of blame she endured when she clearly was not the guilty one! There will never be another pair like those two. Chow and Lizzie, you are so missed!

Betsy Sue

Oh Betsy! What an angel! I wanted a black Labradoodle. I don't know why; don't ask me, but I wanted one. So after a search on the internet, I found a breeder near Pittsburgh, and in time, there was a black, little girl available. It just so happened that Cheryl was going to Pittsburgh to take a class, so she would be the first to meet her and would bring her to her temporary home. From the get-go, Betsy Sue was a pickle. Once again, Harry had the opportunity to introduce another dog to life living in a church, and since he was such a good boy, he helped teach Betsy the finer points of doing "atta-girl" outside! With Harrison's help, she was so easy to train; every time he went out, she went out. She was house-trained in two weeks!

But as far as other training was concerned, I was going to need help. Betsy stayed in the Educational Building and she was a good dog, but we were having trouble walking her, plus she was getting aggressive with people. This was totally out of character for both breeds that were a part of who she was, and it was beginning to be a problem. There were several people who walked her, so we all decided to take her to a dog class, or should I say, Betsy took us to a people class.

At the class the very wonderful trainer taught us how to walk her. We all tried with relative success, except she would not listen to me. The trainer looked at me and said, "You're the problem." Somehow, I knew she was right; she was my baby. The situation began to escalate when the one young man who was helping to walk her had his school schedule changed and was no longer available… and Betsy was a big girl. I could not walk her and she needed exercise. It was obvious that Betsy had too many bosses, and she really did not know who to listen to.

In the meantime, I was feeling guilty about buying this dog. I had made a huge mistake, and so I decided to try to sell her or give her to someone who could better care for her. She needed a strong daddy and a family. She was a dear and needed kids to romp with and a firm hand to guide her through her teenage years.

Then I had a thought, yet I knew this family was not actively seeking a dog… but it was worth a try. I called Kevin and Melissa Wilson who lived next to the church and asked if we could talk. We sat down to talk, and I explained the pickle we were in and point blank said, "Would you be interested in taking Betsy?" Kevin had a strange grin on his face that turned into a laugh. Apparently, they had recently had a conversation about possibly getting a dog, and Kevin's reply was, "I'm only interested in getting a dog like Betsy." It was a done deal. The next day, after work and after they talked to their boys, Betsy moved next door. What a relief and what a *perfect* fit for this family. Betsy is fully a Wilson now, but still recognizes me as her mom. When I visit them, she never knows where to sit, but most of the time, she's beside me leaning into my legs while I spoil her and love on her. She has become a wonderful pet and loves her mommy and daddy and two brothers! Betsy Balooga, you are a doll!

Sadie Anne

After Lucy died, I was truly heartbroken. My dream dog, my brindle Cairn Terrier, my little love bug was gone. It would be impossible to ever hope to replace her. I did some searching, but kept running into the same thing. Everyone told me female brindles are very hard to find. They are usually scooped up from breeders by puppy mills, especially in Pennsylvania. But after an internet search, I found a breeder outside of Mechanicsburg that said she had a litter of brindles. I was thrilled. They weren't ready to be weaned yet, but I could look at them. Before I went, a new couple in the church told me they had seen a brindle Cairn at a pet store in Chambersburg. I firmly explained that I was not buying from a pet store and that was that!

At this time, Bishop Miller was still living in the church, but was starting to fail, and we were not far from having to move her to a facility which could better assist her. These were tough times. On top of that, other situations occurred, and I admit that I needed a doggy kiss every now and then. As I said, tough times. Emotional times. I needed a hug—a hug from a dog, and I didn't have one that was mine to hug.

So on a Saturday, Aunt Cheryl and I travelled to the breeder's home to see the puppies. Oh, they had puppies alright! Puppies which, first of all, were not brindles. Second, puppies that were living in deplorable conditions! I would not even touch them. The breeder kept apologizing for the dirt and the stench, but I was out of there. My heart was broken.

We headed home, and on the way home, Cheryl said, "I know you don"t want to buy from a pet store, but should we just go and check this other dog… just in case?" I wasn't sure; I was pretty emotional. All those puppies, not receiving proper care… I wanted to call the authorities on them, and I eventually did. But out of desperation, I said a tentative, "Okay, let's go," and so we did.

I had my total guard up when we walked into that pet store. But then it took Cheryl about two seconds to find the most beautiful brindle Cairn I had ever seen in her temporary home. She took a look at us and demanded that she be picked up, and within minutes, we were holding this loving ball of fur that was lavishing us with the best puppy kisses ever! When you placed her on the ground, all she wanted to do was play, but as soon as you picked her up, she went limp in your arms and begged to be snuggled. Could this be my new best friend? We spent time with her, then found out the price, and walked out the door.

I thought about her and prayed; the next day was Sunday, and I put my own little fleece before God. "If she's still there Monday morning, I'm going to go get her." Toward 5:00 p.m. on Sunday, when I knew the pet store would close for the day, I was getting very nervous. *Had I made a mistake? What if someone bought her?* But I had prayed, and if she was still there, she was mine. I couldn't control myself. At five minutes before 5:00 p.m., I called the pet store to enquire if she had been purchased. After the longest wait in history, the clerk returned to the phone. She said, "I had to check. We had a ton of people looking at her today, but, yes, she's still here. However, we close in five minutes."

"No problem," I said. "I will try to get there first thing in the morning." Ha! *Try?* The next day *before* they opened, Kimberly and I were sitting in the car waiting to bust in those doors when we saw that latch open.

She was mine. I named her Sadie, after my great-grandmother, and she is an absolutely wonderful dog. But why am I surprised? I believe my steps are ordered by the Lord, and she has been a wonderful delight the last few years as I transitioned through some major life changes—a change in where I live and some truly trying times. She never talks back, and believe it or not, she knows when I am upset, because she jumps on my lap, demands a hug, and showers me with the best kisses ever. Bishop Miller had only a few months to enjoy her, and Sadie visited her twice in the nursing home. Once again, this little dog has also woven herself into the life blood of our church and has managed to play ball with every person who sits down anywhere near her. She has become the "alpha" dog in the pack, she bosses Harry around all the time, and he just looks at her and says, "Yes, dear." I think he's learned some things through the years!

So, this is the on-going saga of another part of our history; I could not leave this "tail" out. Our dogs have walked onto the platform during ballet worship dances, and one time Holly came up the Jubilant Hall stairs and walked down the aisle at Conference while Bishop Beninate was preaching. They've been in every year-end review and have taught each of us lesson after lesson. Bishop Miller often told us, "God can teach you a lot as you learn to care for something alive that depends on you for their existence. And how you care for them speaks of who you really are inside."

Our dogs have helped to make our church a home. If that ever changes, it would be a dog-gone shame!

*Named after the beloved dog of our neighbor!

Me and Libby

Joanie with Holly as a puppy

Beautiful Vinee and beautiful Aunt Cheryl

Lucy, Harry, and Holly

Chow and Lizzie with Joanie

Betsy Sue Wilson

Sadie

A true, incredible story by
Elvina E. Miller, D.D.

Captured in Africa can be purchased for $10.00 each by sending a check for that amount to :

Captured
@Oasis of Love Church
PO Box 38
Shippensburg, PA 17257

Postage is included in the price, except for those who live outside the continental USA.

Call for details to 717-532-5112.

Author Page

Born and raised in Mifflin County, Pennsylvania, Nancy A. Hudson graduated from Chief Logan High School and later from Salem College in West Virginia, with a double major in Art and Oral Communications.

She is the general overseer of the Oasis of Love Churches in Pennsylvania and the Living Fellowship in Arizona, and is the senior pastor of the Oasis of Love Church in Shippensburg, Pennsylvania. The Oasis of Love Church is a vibrant, active, Christian Church that reaches out to the needy in every sphere of society, transforming lives and enabling people to become productive members of the church and community.

A lover of protocol and an advocate for practicing etiquette in every aspect of life, Nancy is a trainer, certified by the Protocol School of Washington.

As a living, techni-color example of loyalty and servanthood, Nancy has served the Founder of the Oasis Churches, Bishop Elvina E, Miller D.D., faithfully since 1974. Paul had his Timothy, Moses had his Joshua, Elijah had his Elisha, and Bishop Miller had her Nancy.

Known for her creativity and innovation, Nancy has continually brought fresh ideas and spearheaded challenging projects, which have motivated and promoted many in the local church to higher heights and deeper levels of commitment. She deftly mixes her love of music, drama, humor, and dance in her presentation of the Gospel to create an inviting environment for the congregation to experience and partake of the Living Word of God.

Some of Nancy's other interests include interior decorating, entertaining, road trips, and… she loves to cook. Many in the fold feel she should try out for "Chopped," but she says she doesn't have time! She is an avid dog person and a general lover of all animals. A sports enthusiast as well, she is an "all-in" Penn State fan, loves the Philadelphia Eagles, Phillies, and Flyers, as well as the Golden State Warriors. With such a wide variety of interests, Nancy relates well with every generation, and much like the Apostle Paul learned through his missionary travels, Nancy has learned through the local church environment, to become all things to all men and women!

You can contact Nancy at: hollywootwee@comcast.net

www.oasisoflove.net

On Facebook as Nancy A. Hudson

On Instagram as Nancy Hudson/sadiebunts10

On Twitter as Nancy A Hudson @NancyAHudson

By Snail Mail: Oasis of Love Church - Nancy A. Hudson - PO Box 38 - Shippensburg, PA 17257

eGenCo

Generation Culture Transformation
Specializing in publishing for generation culture change

Visit us Online at:
www.egen.co

Write to: eGenCo
824 Tallow Hill Road
Chambersburg, PA 17202 USA
Phone: 717-461-3436
Email: info@egen.co

 facebook.com/egenbooks

 youtube.com/egenpub

 egen.co/blog

 twitter.com/egen_co

 instagram.com/egen.co

 pinterest.com/eGenDMP